CA
GOLD
RUSH

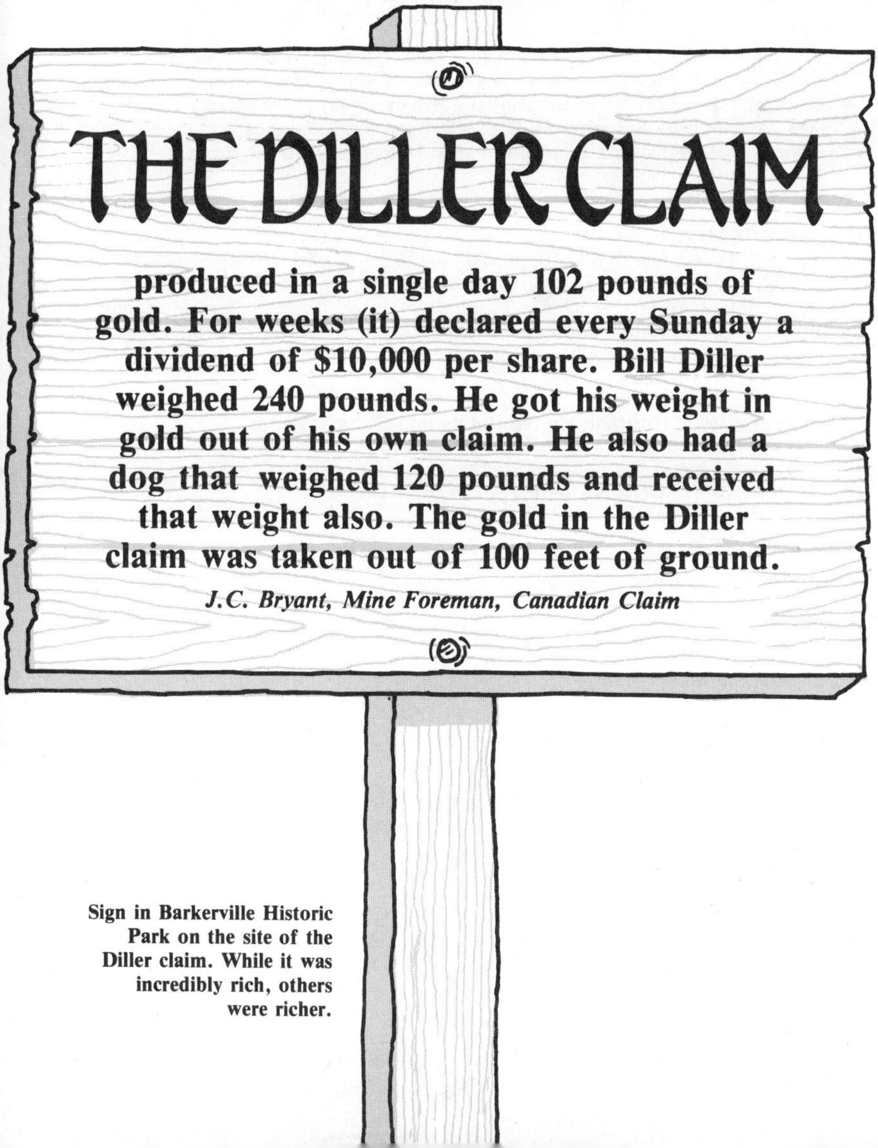

Sign in Barkerville Historic Park on the site of the Diller claim. While it was incredibly rich, others were richer.

BACK COVER
The creek which the miners followed to the Cariboo Plateau is now called Keithley after "Doc" Keithley, one of the original discoverers.

The painting is of Hudson's Bay Company Governor George Simpson and his voyageurs shooting Fraser River rapids above Yale in 1828 while exploring the river as a means of transporting Company supplies. He summarized the dangerous journey in two sentences:

"I should consider the passage down, to be certain Death, in nine attempts out of Ten. I shall therefore no longer talk of it as a navigable stream."

INSIDE BACK COVER
The *Beaver* off Fort Victoria in 1846 and Governor George Simpson being welcomed by James Douglas at Fort St. James in 1828. In 1858 James Douglas became the first governor of the Crown Colony of British Columbia which became a province in 1871.
Both paintings by A. Sheriff Scott, courtesy of Hudson's Bay Company.

COVER ARTIST
John Innes (1864-1941) came to B.C. before the completion of the Canadian Pacific Railway. He developed an interest in history and over the years became very famous for his many paintings of pioneer days in Western Canada. Among them is a series on B.C. which the Native Sons of B.C., Post No 2, had printed as a set of post cards. One is on the front cover.

PHOTO CREDITS
B.C. Provincial Archives: 6-7, 10, 15, 20, 24, 28-29, 32, 35, 38, 43, 50-51, 53, 56, 59, 63, 66, 67, 70, 71, 74, 76, 77, 79, 81, 82, 85; Glenbow Foundation: 56, 70-71; Heritage House: 14-15, 28, 32, 56, 71, 88, back cover, top; McCord Museum: inside front cover; Public Archives of Canada: 42, 43; Tourism B.C.: 11, 94; Vancouver City Archives: 46; Vancouver Public Library: 34-35, 38, 43, 47.

CANADIAN CATALOGUING IN PUBLICATION DATA

Main entry under title:

Gold Rush to Cariboo

ISBN 0-919214-90-8

1. Cariboo (B.C.: Regional district) — Gold discoveries. 2. Fraser River Valley (B.C.) — Gold discoveries.
FC3822.5.G6 1987 972.1′2 C87-091038-8 F1089.C3G6 1987

HERITAGE HOUSE PUBLISHING COMPANY LTD.
Unit #8 17921 55 Ave., Surrey, B.C. V3S 6C4

Printed in Canada

PRINTING HISTORY
First Edition: 1987
Reprinted: 1994

CONTENTS

THE COVER

The Discovery of Gold on Williams Creek in 1861, from a painting by renowned B.C. artist John Innes and reproduced courtesy Native Sons of B.C., Post No. 2.

Williams Creek proved to be not only the richest of all the Cariboo streams but, for its size, among the world's richest. It was discovered by M.C. Brown, J. Costello and William Dietz. After the gold rush Brown gave the following account of its discovery and naming:

"We crossed the divide, eventually making the headwaters of the creek, after some tiresome travelling, down which we travelled to a place near a little gulch or canyon, where we camped for the night, building a brush shelter.

"On the following morning we separated to prospect the stream, agreeing to meet again at night to report progress. The story of that day's prospecting, which we recalled over the camp fire, has become a matter of mining history in British Columbia. 'Dutch Bill' made the best prospect, striking pay dirt going $1.25 a pan. I and Costello had also done pretty well, finding dirt worth a dollar or so a pan. You can well imagine we were well pleased with our day's exertions, and each man in his heart felt that we had discovered very rich ground. I shall not forget the discussion that took place as to the name to be given the creek. Dutch Bill was for having it called 'Billy Creek' because he had found the best prospects of the three. I was quite agreeable, but I stipulated that Mr. William Dietz should buy the first basket of champagne that reached the creek. This appealed to Costello, and so the creek was then and there named — not Billy Creek, but 'Williams Creek.' "

AMONG THE CONTRIBUTORS

The six chapters describing the 1858 stampede to the Fraser River and subsequent discovery of the gold-laden creeks in the Cariboo Mountains are excerpted from *British Columbia — Historical Volume Two*. This massive series on B.C.'s earliest history was published in 1914, its authors Judge F.W. Howay and Provincial Librarian-Archivist E.O.S. Scholefield.

Judge Howay (1867-1943) was born in New Westminster. He taught school in Ladner before switching to law, was appointed to the County Court in 1907 and spent thirty years as a judge. His career as a judge and as an author resulted in many awards and appointments, including Chairman of the Historic Sites and Monuments Board of Canada and President of the Canadian Historical Society. When he died the Canadian government named a peak in the Stave Lake area near Vancouver Mount Judge Howay in his honor.

E.O.S. Scholefield (1875-1919) was born in England but educated in Victoria. In 1894 he joined the staff of the Provincial Library and began a distinguished career. In 1898 he became Provincial Librarian and in 1910 also Provincial Archivist.

In a few years he transformed the Provincial Library, adding some 50,000 titles in the first fourteen years he held office. He was especially interested in Northwest history, obtaining many collections of manuscripts, books and newspapers for the Archives. Today the newspaper collection contains almost every edition of every paper published in the province. In addition, the Archives has some 500,000 historical photos, among much other material.

Scholefield was only forty-four when he died after a long illness. Many people felt his illness in part resulted from the long hours he spent as custodian of B.C.'s Provincial Library and Archives.

William G.R. Hind (1833-1889), whose painting of miners at Lillooet in 1865 is on the inside front cover, was very familiar with his subject. He was one of the Overlanders of 1862, a group of 150 men and a pregnant woman with three children who left Eastern Canada for the Cariboo in 1862. It was an epic journey. On June 2 they left Fort Garry (now Winnipeg) in ox-drawn Red River carts. The first 900 miles to Fort Edmonton they covered fairly quickly since they averaged 2 1/2 miles an hour. But then for much of the route westward there wasn't even a trail. The Overlanders abandoned their carts and used horses and oxen as pack animals.

When their journey ended more than three months later several were dead, the rest lucky to survive. Their venture was summarized thus by one of them: "Our mining tools were the only articles . . . that we found to be unnecessary." (See Heritage House book, *The Overlanders of '62*.)

Hind established a studio in Victoria and remained in B.C. for about seven years, then returned to the Maritimes where he died suddenly at fifty-six. He was a solitary man who seldom bothered to sign his work. Until recently he was almost forgotten but today is considered among the best of Canada's early artists. Many of his paintings and sketches are in the Public Archives of Canada and B.C.'s Provincial Archives which bought a series found in the attic of an old house in Nova Scotia.

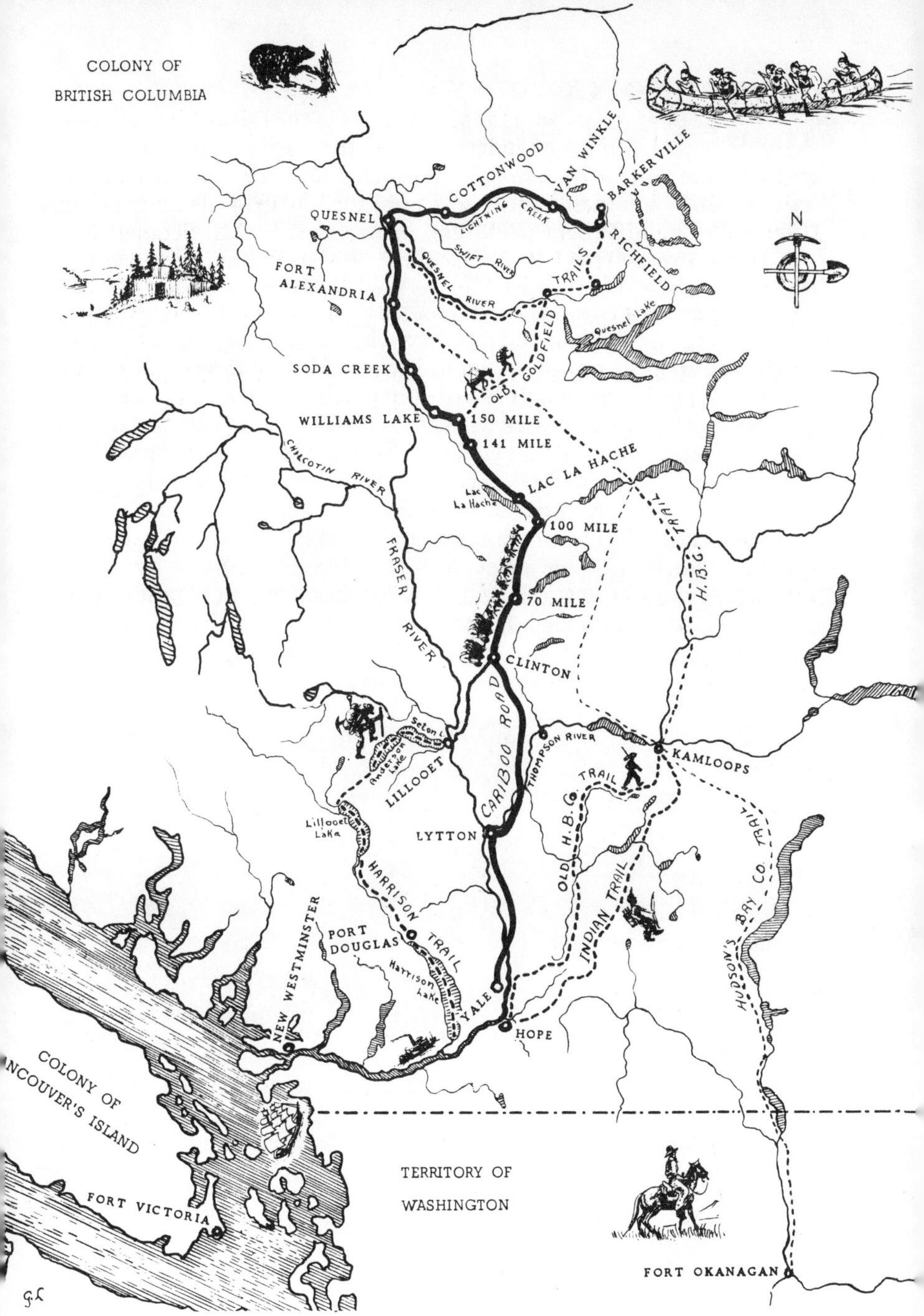

THE CARIBOO WAGON ROAD IN 1865

Route of the Cariboo Wagon Road in 1865, with some of the main Hudson's Bay Company trails and early miners' routes to the goldfields. At the beginning of the rush each party found its own way to the creeks, resulting in many individual trails through the wilderness.

Stampede to Fraser River Gold

Who discovered placer gold in British Columbia? And when? and where? Perhaps no questions concerning our past have been so much debated.

Chief Trader McLean at Kamloops is alleged to have procured gold dust from the natives as early as 1852. This is supported by Gavin Hamilton, a Chief Factor of the Hudson's Bay Company, but in reference to a later year. He says it "is absolutely certain that gold was discovered in the Thompson River during the season of 1856, because Mr. McLean at Kamloops had two pint pickle bottles half full of gold taken from the river that year."

Roderick Finlayson [an HBC Chief Factor who in 1843 assisted in founding Fort Victoria] claimed that gold was discovered on the Thompson River and that Chief Trader McLean sent to Victoria for iron spoons to be used in extracting the nuggets from the crevices of the bedrock. James Houston of Langley claimed to be the discoverer of gold in British Columbia. His story was that in 1854 he came from the Columbia River by way of Okanagan, and stopped at the Hudson's Bay Company's old post at Tranquille Creek, near Kamloops. In the following month, to the astonishment of all the men there, he found coarse gold near the point where the Tranquille empties into the Thompson. This gold he sent to Governor Douglas,

and it was, according to Mr. Houston, the first intimation that officer had of the existence of placer gold on the Mainland.

Wherever gold was first found in British Columbia, there is little doubt that the discovery which brought the Fraser region into notice, and hence is claimed by many as the original discovery, was made on the Nicomen River which flows into the Thompson a few miles east of Lytton. Governor Douglas in his diary says: "Gold was first found on Thompson River by an Indian a quarter of a mile below Nicomen. He is since dead. The Indian was taking a drink out of the river; having no vessel he was quaff-

Among the thousands of miners was Edward Stout. In 1858 his party of twenty-five was attacked by Indians in the Fraser Canyon. Only five survived, Stout hit by seven arrows. He recovered and was one of the group which discovered Williams Creek, the richest of all the golden streams. He died in 1924 at Yale age ninety-nine and is commemorated by Stouts Gulch at Barkerville.

Below: The Fraser River, whose rapids drowned scores of miners, and the Hudson's Bay Company's steamer *Otter*. In February 1858 she carried 800 ounces of gold to the San Francisco mint and started the rush to Fraser River.

ing from the stream when he perceived a shining pebble which he picked up, and it proved to be gold. The whole tribe forthwith began to collect the glittering metal. This was likely in 1856."

American adventurers began to resort to the country with the first news of gold discoveries. In 1857 they made their way from the Columbia into the watershed of the Thompson River. The natives, having learned the value of the yellow metal, threatened to prevent all attempts at mining on any of the tributaries of the Thompson. The miners, nevertheless, entered that territory, prospected the streams, and found gold. The great area covered by them in these researches gave ground for a well-founded opinion that the whole territory was gold bearing. In December 1857, Governor Douglas reported: "The reputed wealth of the Couteau mines [the local name for the Thompson-Fraser River area] is causing much excitement amongst the population of the United States of Washington and Oregon, and I have no doubt that a great number of people from those territories will be attracted thither in spring."

[The Governor's prediction quickly became fact, triggered by the action of the Hudson's Bay Company. By now the Indians had mined about 800 ounces of gold and traded it to the HBC. Since the gold was no use in its raw state and the nearest mint was in San Francisco, the HBC shipped it south on the steamship *Otter* in February 1858. The news quickly spread and in March a vanguard of prospectors arrived on the Fraser River. A few miles above Fort Hope they discovered rich pay on a bar they named Hill's after the man who washed the first gold. News of their success and samples of the gold were back in San Francisco by April, and the rush started to Fraser River.]

Fortune beckoned to the downhearted of Oregon and California, and pointed towards the yellow star now rising above the unknown wild of New Caledonia. [The name during the fur-trade era for what is today Central B.C.] The lure of the gold is always strong; in these circumstances it was irresistible. The excitement increased daily. As Donald Fraser, the *Times* correspondent, wrote: "None too poor and none too rich to go. None too young and none too old to go; even the decrepit go." Rumour painted the Couteau country as a second California or Australia in point of mineral wealth.

From the Territory of Washington, boats, canoes, and every species of small craft poured their human cargoes into the Fraser River District. On Puget Sound shipping was paralyzed. All the crews deserted and rushed en masse to make their fortunes in the mines. All manufacturing, all industry was at a standstill. No ties were strong enough to resist the golden influences. Even the soldiers in United States posts of Steilacoom, Forts Townsend and Bellingham deserted in numbers. But in California the excitement was, if possible, even more intense. On April 25th, the *Commodore* arrived from San Francisco with 450 miners. Governor Douglas reported on May 8th that "Not less than one thousand whites are already at work and on the way to the gold districts." A week later he increased his estimate, stating that "fifteen hundred white miners, at the smallest computation, had reached the diggings." All through the month of May vessels of every size and kind sailed from San Francisco laden with eager treasure seekers.

[During April, May, June and July, 16,144 people left San Francisco for the Fraser River, most landing at Fort Victoria. The greatest crowd leaving San Francisco on any one day was 1,723 on July 3rd, but July 10th was fairly close when 1,409 embarked.]

The enumeration given only relates to the emigration through San Francisco. It may be added that these official figures are much smaller than the numbers which common report stated were being carried by the various vessels. For comparison, the following are given: On July 1st, the *Sierra Nevada* landed 1,900; on July 8th the *Orizaba* and the *Cortez* together brought 2,800. [The latter had officially taken on board only 1,300 passengers.] We may safely conclude that every vessel was carrying without regard to coasting laws or safety, all who wished to embark. How nearly the reported numbers approached the actual numbers can only be surmised. With the necessary allowance in this respect and with the addition of those who came from Oregon and Washington, from St. Paul, from Salt Lake City, and other western points, from the Hawaiian Islands and the various ports of Central and Southern America, it is perhaps fair to say that at least 25,000 persons were borne on that tide.

The scene in California is thus described: "The roads from the mountains were lined with foot-passengers on their way to San Francisco. Stage coaches came rolling into Sacramento, groaning under their living cargo of sturdy miners. The worm-eaten wharves of San Francisco trembled almost daily under the tread of the vast multitudes that gathered to see a northern steamer leave. With that reckless disregard of human life so characteristic of the American ship-owner, old hulks, which had long been known to be unseaworthy and rotten, were refitted for the new El Dorado. Engines, rusty from years of idleness, were polished up; leaky boilers were repatched — paint and putty filling gaping seams; and with names often changed to hide their former reputations, steamer after steamer sailed from our port, loaded to the guards with freight, and black with the crowds who were rushing to the newly-discovered land of gold."

As the Reverend R.C. Lundin Brown says, "In short, never in the history of the migrations of men has been seen such a 'rush', so sudden and so fast."

The newspapers eagerly sought for and published every scrap of information about the mines. The excited public avidly devoured every item. In April, the *Pioneer and Democrat*, a newspaper published in Olympia, Washington, stated that within a few months the Hudson's Bay Company had traded with the Indians 110 pounds of coarse gold procured from surface workings with crude implements. The same issue stated that between 150 and 200 miners were already at work on the Fraser, and that 3 men had obtained $800 as the result of 10 days' work.

The early arrivals were not slow in sending out glowing accounts of the prospects. These were read even more greedily than the newspapers. The following are reproduced as samples:

"Fraser River Gold Mines,
April 29, 1858

"FRIEND PLIMMER:

"We have arrived in these mines at last, after one of the hardest trips

A sketch of Fort Yale that appeared in *Harper's Weekly* on October 9, 1858. By 1859 the miners had battled up the Fraser River, opposite, and discovered that its canyons and rapids extended hundreds of miles northward from Lillooet.

on record. I shall not attempt to give you a narrative of the difficulties and dangers of travelling on this river, as it would be impossible for me to do justice to it at present. It was next to impossible to get up when we came, and when the river rises to its full height no canoe or boat can possibly get up or down.

"We are now located thirty miles above the junction of the Fraser and Thompson rivers, on Fraser River. The distances up are as follows: From the mouth of Fraser River to Fort Langley, thirty miles; from there to Fort Hope, sixty miles; from Fort Hope to Fort Yale, one day's travel; from Fort Yale to the Forks, eight days' travel, and from the Forks to where we are now, thirty miles; making in all about two hundred miles. About one-fourth of the canoes that attempt to come up are lost in the rapids, which extend from Fort Yale nearly to the Forks. A few days ago six men were drowned by their canoe being upset in attempting to go down. There is more danger in going down than in coming up. There can be no doubt about this country being immensely rich in gold. Almost every bar on the river from Fort Yale up will pay from $3 to $7 a day to the man, at the present stage of the water, and when the river gets low, which will be about next August, they will pay very well. One hundred and ninety-six dollars was taken out by one man last winter in a few hours, but the water was then at its lowest stage. The gold in the bars is all very fine and hard to save in a rocker, but with quicksilver properly managed, good wages can be made almost anywhere on the river as long as the bars are not actually covered with water. We have not been able to find a place yet where we

can work anything but rockers; if we could get a sluice to work here we could make from $12 to $16 a day each. We only commenced work yesterday, and we are satisfied when we get fully under way we can make from $5 to $7 per day each. The prospect is better as we go up the river on the bars. The gold is not any coarser, but there is more of it. There are men at work here who have been thirty miles higher up and who say they made from $10 to $16 a day and that it can be made on high bars where the water will not trouble them until it obtains its highest point. There is also in that region diggings of coarser gold on small streams that empty into the main river; a few men have been there and proved the existence of rich diggings by bringing specimens back with them. The Indians all along the river from Fort Hope have a considerable quantity of gold in their possession that they say they dug themselves, but those above us will not point out the place where they get it, nor allow small parties of men to go up to look after it. I have seen pieces in their possession that weighed two pounds. The Indians on the river as far up as where we are have been very friendly, and I presume they will remain so, but those above us are disposed to be troublesome. We have been twenty miles above here on a bar which was paying $15 a day, but the Indians went into camp about a mile above us and forcibly took the provisions and arms from a party of four men and cut two of the party severely with their knives in the row. They came into our camp the same day and insisted that we should trade with them or leave their country. All the white men that were settled along the river in that section collected together, and, as the bar there was not large enough for us all to work on, all hands moved down here. This bar is large enough for a hundred men to work on all summer; there are now about forty men on it.

"We design at present to remain here until we can get one hundred men together, when we will move up above the Falls and do just about what we please without regard to the Indians. There can be no doubt about the existence of rich mines of coarse gold in many parts of this country, but there have not been men enough here yet to even prospect it. We are at present the highest up of any party of white men on the river, and we must go higher to be satisfied. Five or six dollar diggings won't do while there is better in the country. I don't apprehend any danger from the Indians at present, but there will be hell to pay after a while. [His words were prophetic. Miners by the score were murdered by the Indians when war erupted during the summer of 1858.]

"We are determined to remain here, if possible, until the river falls, when good diggings can be found anywhere. I would not advise anybody to come here until about the last of July, when I think they can get up the river without much difficulty. There is a pack trail from Fort Hope, but it cannot be travelled until the snow is off the mountains.

"The prices of provisions here are as follows: flour, $35 per cwt.; pork, $1 per lb.; beans, 50 cents per lb., and other things in proportion. Every party that starts from the Sound should have their own supplies to last them three or four months, and should bring the largest sized Chinook canoes, as small ones are liable to swamp in the rapids. Each canoe should be provided with about thirty fathoms of strong line for towing over swift water, and every man well armed. The Indians here can beat anything alive stealing, and if they continue to improve in that art, they will soon be able to steal a man's food after he has eaten it. We have lost nothing so far but a little sugar, but others have suffered severely. We are all in good health and spirits and expect to make a raise here before we leave. We have all promised to write to different persons in Seattle, but this will have to do for all at present.

"Yours truly,
"FRANKLIN MATTHIAS."

"To R.R. Rees, Portland, Oregon
May 28, 1858.

"I am now on Fraser River, not far from Fort Yale, and am mining; and I suppose you have heard various reports from these mines. As far as I know, they are as good as I have ever seen. The river is very high now and rising fast, and we have to work on the highest bars, yet make from $12 to $50 to each rocker, so you may know what we can do when the river falls. We have sluices, also, although the gold is very fine and we lose much of it without quicksilver. Now, if you want to come here, I will say this — that this is the best mining region that I have ever yet seen; and I want you to tell Wm. Bridge to come with goods if he wants to come, for everything commands a high price here, etc. Be sure and write to him and tell him to start by the first of July, or any time, as I presume he can come where we are at any time; and if he has anything for sale he can sell it here at almost his own terms; and tell all my friends in Portland the contents of this letter, etc. Tell them that we are now working entirely on the river bars, and go down from two inches to two feet and make $8 to $50 — or I may say from $6 to $50; and if you come and don't find it as I say, I am here — take any revenge; but don't let any other reports prevent you if you start.

"Come if you come at all, to Olympia; there purchase a good canoe, and get you some Indians and come right along, and you will find us eight miles from Fort Yale.

"S. ALLEN"

Each incoming vessel spoke of hundreds of adventurers chafing restlessly in San Francisco, anxiously awaiting an opportunity to obtain passage to the new gold fields. Lieutenant Mayne, [a British Naval Officer at Esquimalt near Fort Victoria on what was then the Colony of Vancouver's Island] speaking of this period, says: "That road, too, from Esquimalt to Victoria, about which so much has since been said, in and out of the Colonial Assembly, was changed with the rest almost beyond recognition. Only a few months before, we used to flounder through the mud without meeting a single soul; now it was covered with pedestrians toiling along, with the step and air of men whose minds are occupied with thoughts of business; crowded with well-laden carts and vans, with Wells Fargo's or Freeman's 'Expresses' and with strangers of every tongue and country, in every variety of attire. Day after day on they came to Victoria, on their way to the Fraser; the greater part of them with no property but the bundle they carried, and with 'dollars, dollars, dollars!' stamped on every face."

The majority of those who sailed from San Francisco debarked at Victoria, though some went on to ports on Puget Sound. Wherever they landed about two hundred miles lay between them and the mining region. The greatest of their difficulties were before them. There were no regular means of communication with the Fraser River, and they were compelled for the first two or three months to make their way as best they could, either by boats or canoes or some kind of sailing vessel, to its mouth. The treacherous waters of the Strait of Georgia took their toll. Many were never heard of after leaving Victoria. But nothing daunted them. They battled the fierce tide-rips and the sudden gales with grim determination. Even after they entered the river, troubles and dangers were their lot. The freshet-swollen stream opposed their advance.

Speaking on this subject, in May, Governor Douglas said: "Many accidents have happened in the dangerous rapids of that river; a great number of canoes having been dashed to pieces and their cargoes swept away by the impetuous stream, while of the ill-fated adventurers who accompanied them, many have been swept into eternity." Yet during the first week of June fifty canoes, containing an average of six persons, reached Fort Hope in safety.

Northward up Fraser River

Early in August [1858] difficulties with the Indians forced the miners above Yale to flee in terror to that place. Those who saved their lives were robbed of tools and provisions — a serious loss, indeed, at that time. Many were unable to make their escape, and their bodies, in some instances scalped, came floating down the raging river. The cause of the trouble was a combination of influences: the desire of the Indians to monopolize the mining, the successes of the Indians in the war in Washington then in progress, the arrogance of the miners, especially the American miners, who acted as though the Indian had no rights, and, lastly, the interference with the Indian women. The natives were reported to be obtaining firearms and firewater from the Chinese.

A rifle company of forty was organized by Captain Rouse and set out with packs on their backs on August 9th to force a passage to the Forks [Lytton]. The details of the movements of this company are variously

At the 6,000-foot level of the Cariboo Mountains snow lingers until July or later and can return by September. The peaks below are part of the Snowshoe Plateau, headwaters of Antler, Williams, Cunningham, Keithley and other creeks whose gravel yielded gold by the ton.

Richard Willoughby, bottom, discovered Lightning Creek which yielded nuggets up to 10 ounces. Contrary to many miners who dug a fortune but died penniless, Willoughby left an estate of over $100,000 when he died in 1904.

reported, but it appears that, reaching the Rancheria [Spuzzum], they engaged in a contest with the Indians in which some seven of the latter were killed; continuing in their work of destruction they burned three Indian villages and attacked the natives wherever they met them.

The storm centre was the Big Canyon [Hells Gate]. There a large body of savages congregated, taking possession of the points of vantage with the intention of barring the further advance of the whites. The trouble could scarcely have occurred at a more opportune time. The population of Yale, incuding the refugees, was in excess of three thousand, all waiting like owners of tickets in some great lottery for the drawing to commence. A meeting of nearly two thousand was held. A call for volunteers was issued, and responded.

Opinions were divided as to the course to be pursued. Forty of the volunteers selected Graham as their commander, and determined to follow a policy of extermination; but the remainder, believing in conciliation and sufficient exhibition of force to obtain this end, placed themselves under H. M. Snyder as captain. In the fort was a case of rifles; at first Mr. Allard, the [Hudson's Bay] company's officer in charge, refused to supply these weapons, but as matters now assumed a more threatening attitude the miners demanded and obtained them. Captain Snyder induced the "war-to-the-knife" faction to lag behind to enable him to settle matters.

Leaving Yale on August 18th with one hundred and twenty-three volunteers and provisions for five days, Captain Snyder made his course up the river. At Spuzzum reinforcements joined his party. At China Bar the party were surprised to find some five miners in a sort of a fortification. Amongst these persons was Edward Stout, one of the earliest of the pioneer miners. This party, which had originally consisted of twenty-five miners, had been well to the forefront in the ascent of the river, had then advanced through the canyons to Lytton, and thence up the Thompson, prospecting and mining as they went. Warned of the hostile intentions of the natives, they had stealthily made their way down the river, avoiding the usual lines of travel, but, in spite of the utmost precautions, their movements were discovered and they were harassed by a running fire. Man by man was picked off by bullet or Indian arrow until but five were left, and of these scarcely one but bore wounds more or less severe.

The display of force had its effect. Treaties of peace and amity were concluded with all the chiefs between Yale and Lytton, including Spintlum, a noted Thompson River chief. The expedition under Snyder returned on August 25th, accompanied by five of the chiefs, having established peace on that portion of the river. Only two men were lost on the undertaking — Captain Graham and his lieutenant, the leaders of the extermination section, who were shot by Indians at Long Bar for having trampled down a flag of truce. With news of the satisfactory adjustment of the trouble the miners streamed out of Yale to reoccupy their ground and be ready to take advantage of the expected fall of the waters.

In August the long looked for fall of the river commenced; between the 5th and the 12th it fell four feet and a half at Yale. But hope was doomed to disappointment. Again the waters rose, and a further period of enforced delay occurred. The river was struggling desperately to retain its wealth.

About the end of August the real fall began. In a few days 200 men were at work on Fort Yale Bar, and 400 on Hill's Bar.

Like peaks above the deluge, the bars began to appear with the gradual recession and were greedily seized upon by the waiting hundreds. Miners were now scattered all along the river from Fort Langley to Pavilion Creek, the northerly boundary of the Couteau country, a distance of about 200 miles. The mining was still almost entirely bar mining. These bars were merely the exposed river bottom — sandy flats occurring in the river bends. For ages the Fraser, rushing madly along, had torn away the gold-bearing rock, crushed it in its natural setting and deposited the gold with its accompanying metallic sand in the eddies in these bends.

With the recession of the water these bars became the scenes of great activity. Although in the painful interval of waiting — June to September — thousands had left the country and, notwithstanding that the size of a claim was but twenty-five feet square, the bars below the canyon were overcrowded. There was no bed-rock in these sands, but there was, nevertheless, a recognized pay stratum, clearly defined and differing in color from the worthless sand of the bar. This auriferous deposit was sometimes situated a few inches below the surface, at other places it was two feet or even more. It also varied in thickness.

On Hill's Bar, it was claimed to have been six feet thick and sixty feet wide, extending the whole length of the bar, a distance of fully half a mile, and yielding on the average 50 cents a pan. As an instance of the richness of this bar, it is recorded that Mr. Winston and two partners took out forty-six pounds of gold dust between December 1858, and April 1859. Frequently they obtained fifty ounces in a day and sometimes, when the sluices were running day and night, seventy to eighty ounces in the same time.

In September, Alfred Waddington counted 800 rockers at work between Fort Hope and Fort Yale. In November, Douglas reported that there were over 10,000 persons engaged in mining, of whom one-half were between Murderer's Bar and Fort Yale. This did not, by any means, indicate that the bars in that locality were the richest; but that access to the diggings above the canyons were so difficult, the supply of food so precarious, and its price so high that all but the most resolute and adventurous were deterred.

It is impossible to enter into the details of the output of the various bars. The total for the six months — June to December, 1858 — was $520,353. Hill's Bar was admitted on all sides to be the richest, and, besides being the first discovered in the advance of 1858, was the longest mined. The other bars, it may be said in a general way, varied in productiveness from those which barely paid meagre wages to those that produced three and four ounces per man per day.

These bars formed but stepping-stones for the restless, roaming miners, who pressed on and on up the river, finding gold wherever they prospected, but never satisfied, striving ever to discover those richer diggings, the existence of which was heresy to deny. [Fort] Alexandria was reached, and then the bars above that place were tested and rich diggings were found in that vicinity. Still "onward" was the cry. By the month of May the Quesnel River [about 400 miles upstream] had been reached. Rumors of great "strikes" there were current. But the Lure of the Gold was strong;

it drew the seekers on. The Fraser was examined and prospected for a distance of one hundred and fifty miles beyond Fort George [today's Prince George]. Every bar was reported as promising from $5 to $6 per day to the man. Better fortune came to those who left the Fraser and ascended the Quesnel.

Late in 1859, after prospecting its bars, which proved far richer than those of the main river, Cariboo Lake was found. In cumbersome rafts, bound together with withes, they made their way along its shores. Now their perseverance was rewarded. Rich strikes, in some cases $200 per day per man, were reported. Gold in large quantities was also found on the Horsefly River, which flows into Quesnel Lake from the southward. There a party of five men in one week with two rockers, took out one hundred and one ounces. One of the foremost in the advance into the Horsefly was Dud Moreland, who later settled at Cottonwood.

Over and above these material results, which showed a large area to be auriferous, and some sections to be especially so, the season of 1859 was eminently satisfactory. In the territory around Quesnel and Cariboo Lakes the California miners found an indication which gladdened their hearts — the "Blue Lead" as it was called, which in California was the gold-bearing stratum. It was traced for thirty miles with a lateral extent of nearly ten miles. It is a question, much debated, whether the real California blue lead existed in British Columbia; but that is beside the point, for the miners believed it did and acted on that assumption. Shafts were sunk to a depth of twenty-five feet to reach the bed-rock, with its covering of blue clay, the alleged blue lead. The results were satisfactory, though the season was too far advanced for any comprehensive attempts.

[During 1860, about four thousand miners were panning and rocking the gravel of creeks and rivers throughout B.C., with some three thousand of them on the Fraser River and its tributaries north of Lillooet. Most found gold, but to those who ventured up the Quesnel River fell the ultimate bonanza. In the fall of 1860 "Doc" Keithley, George Weaver and their companions came across a creek which flowed into Cariboo Lake from a northerly direction. They named it Keithley after its discoverer and headed into the thick underbrush to test its gravel.]

It was the first of the real Cariboo creeks, and soon became one of the most famous, though not at all a rich creek, as compared with its more famous neighbors. The creek itself, as well as its tributary, Snowshoe, and Harvey and Cunningham Creeks, which flow from the eastward face of Bald Mountain, had been discovered early in 1860. But the absence of gold-bearing stratum on the surface had delayed its exploitation, and it was not until late in the fall of that year that its auriferous character was ascertained. It rose at once into prominence as a supply centre for the entire region of the North Quesnel River. The creeks which radiate from Bald Mountain: Keithley, Harvey, Cunningham, Snowshoe, Grouse, Antler, Lowhee, Williams, and Lightning appear to occupy the same location, but not the identical channel of gold-bearing creeks. Where gold was first found on them is said to have been the spot where erosion had laid bare, or nearly bare, for short distances, the deeper channels of the ancient streams.

Late in the fall of 1860, John Rose [who met a tragic death in 1863] and his partner McDonald, with "Doc" Keithley and George Weaver, set out from Keithley Creek in search of new diggings. Ascending that creek for about five miles, they took a course northeastward up a ravine. Reaching Snowshoe Creek, a branch of Keithley, they followed it to its source, some six or seven miles further, near the summit of the watershed dividing the streams flowing into Cariboo Lake from those flowing eastward, northward, and westward into Bear, Willow, and Cottonwood Rivers. Thence the whole surrounding country lay unrolled before them.

Northward and eastward the horizon was bounded by rugged and lofty mountains; towards the west and northwest the prospect was more level; while immediately below lay rolling hills intersected by valleys and ravines. 'Twas man's first view of Cariboo. Over the whole region lay the mantle of solitude and silence — gold existing without contention or struggle. Traversing this summit in the same general direction they came upon another creek, at a distance of about twenty miles from Keithley. The creek [Antler] winds through the centre of a narrow valley and is surmounted by hills sloping down to flats and benches of alluvial deposit. The bed-rock on which gold was found lay but a short distance under the surface, and in many places cropped out. Here was the richest deposit yet found in British Columbia — considerable quantities of gold being found on the bare rock.

One pan produced $25 -- a second, $75. The fortunate prospectors, however, had their ardour somewhat cooled the next morning by awakening to find a foot of snow on the ground. Here, again, besides the actual value of the find, was the strengthening of their faith in the auriferous nature of the country. They found a kind of slate rock covered with red gravel and said to bear a close resemblance to the gold-producing beds of Californian streams. These discoverers tried to keep the secret; but gold, like murder, will out.

Returning to Keithley Creek for provisions, an incautious word at "Red-headed" Davis's store gave the clue. In midwinter, on snowshoes, over four or five feet of snow, miners set out from Keithley to stake the vacant ground on Antler. Many claims were recorded, and, in several instances, the same ground was taken up by different parties. This led to disputes. Mr. Nind, the Gold Commissioner for the district with headquarters at William's Lake, came in over the snow to settle these conflicting claims. Arriving in March 1861, he found, on Antler Creek, one log cabin built by Rose and McDonald. The remainder of the men were living in holes dug in the snow, which was six or seven feet deep. Even under these conditions some prospecting was being carried on, with successful results, though the labor of clearing away the snow and sinking holes to bed-rock was excessive.

The Golden Creeks of Cariboo

But Antler Creek was only the portal of Cariboo, a region studded with mountains of considerable altitude, closely packed together. This creek coursed around the greatest of the three great peaks of Cariboo — Mount Agnes, commonly called Bald Mountain. Impressively grand and sublime are these majestic spurs of the Rockies towering to six and seven thousand feet. The land of Golden Promise, so firmly believed in, so earnestly sought for, lay just on the other side of Mount Agnes, only twelve miles away.

When the mid-winter rush was made upon Antler Creek, a party, amongst whom were Edward Stout, Michael Burns, "Fidele" or Vital, and William Dietz (commonly called Dutch Bill), started in search of other fields. Crossing the ridge which culminates in Mount Agnes, they kept to the northward and descended upon a creek which forms the headwaters of Willow River. This was Williams Creek, the richest, the most celebrated of all the Cariboo creeks. Dutch Bill, its discoverer, after whom it was named, found gold at the canyon about half way between Richfield and Barkerville, as afterwards located.

At first Williams Creek gave no hint of its immense deep-hidden wealth. The canyon where discovery was made was the very poorest part. Dutch Bill's prospecting gave about 75 cents to the pan, yet that was good pay, but in no way suggestive, even to the optimistic, of the world-renowned

The canyon where gold was discovered on Williams Creek proved the poorest section.

The Creeks of Cariboo, showing the present road to Barkerville and the original wagon road from Van Winkle. The first route to the gold-rich region was up the Cariboo River to Keithley Creek, then northward to Snowshoe Creek and the 6,000-foot level of the Cariboo Mountains.

richness of the Steele, the Diller, the Cameron, and the Ericson claims. Returning, the party spread the news of their find, and pellmell went the mad rush to Williams Creek. No roads or trails existed in the Cariboo country at the time, and each party took the course which they judged best, for, as already mentioned, from the tops of the ridges Cariboo was like an open book.

Thus in making from Quesnel River and Keithley Creek to Williams the miners came upon Lightning Creek, which empties into Swift River and Lowhee Creek, flowing into Jack of Clubs Lake. The origins of these names may be of interest. The latter creek was discovered by Richard Willoughby in 1861 and named by him in honor of the "Great Lowhee," a secret society at Yale, in which he was a prominent member. The former owes its name to the following incident. A party, while traveling through its valley, were suddenly overtaken by one of those thunderstorms common in the mountain regions. One of the party, feeling greatly inconvenienced by the severity of the storm — being drenched to the skin — exclaimed aloud, "Boys, this is lightning," feeling fully convinced that this was the most emphatic expression he could use to express his opinion of the inclement weather.

Another version of this story is that "Early in 1861, Bill Cunningham, Jack Hume, and Jim Bell, three gold hunters, started southward over the mountains from Jack of Clubs Creek on a prospecting tour. They found the trip exceedingly rough and laborious, especially in descending the steep banks of the creek they came to. The former called out to his companions, 'Boys, this is lightning,' it being a favourite expression with him in meeting anything difficult to overcome."

Every creek proved to be gold-bearing. The news of their richness lost nothing by repetition and the Fraser, Thompson, and the Rock Creek diggings, which for some time had been gradually falling into the hands of the Chinese, were practically abandoned to them. So the spring and summer of 1861 saw the mountains of Cariboo swarming with eager miners, many of whom had left good diggings in the lower country.

Williams Creek, for a time, gave such poor results that it was called Humbug Creek. During the early summer of 1861 mining was confined to the portion above the canyon. There the pay dirt, the bed of the old creek, lay close to the surface, usually within eight or twelve feet. At that depth, a hard blue clay was met which was supposed to be the bedrock, and upon it good pay was found. But later in that year Mr. Abbott of the Jourdan and Abbott claim, while his partner was away for the day obtaining provisions, concluded to go through this clay and ascertain what lay below. Piercing it, he found below a stratum of gold-bearing gravel, so rich that when his partner returned, after a lapse of forty-eight hours, he produced fifty ounces as the result of his explorations. Up to this time only six claims on the creek had produced gold. With this news all was changed. Hundreds crowded other hundreds in a mad rush.

The whole creek and the hillside for a distance of six miles was literally covered with miners and mining claims, now increased to 100 feet square. The only spot neglected, strange as it may seem, was the spot in the canyon where Dutch Bill had first found gold. But while above the canyon the diggings were shallow, permitting the barren covering to be washed off and the use of sluices and bed-rock flumes, yet below the canyon conditions were totally different. The pay dirt there lay fifty or sixty feet below the present level. Shafts must be sunk, drifts made, and tunnels driven. Pumps would be required to keep the workings dry, and hoisting gear to raise the dirt to the surface to be washed. This work could be carried on throughout the year, while the advent of winter prevented all operations in the surface diggings above the canyon.

Governor Douglas reported that the least Abbott and Jourdan took out, with three men, was one hundred and twenty ounces per day. Judge Begbie reported in September 1861, that the Abbott and Jourdan claim, and the Steele claim, which were both in the shallow diggings above the canyon, were producing thirty to forty pounds of gold per day; and that Steele had informed him that they had taken out in one day three hundred and seventy ounces. The greatest day's yield of the Steele claim in 1861 was four hundred and nine ounces.

On Lowhee, Willoughby, the discoverer, with from four to seven men, between July 27 and September 8, 1861, took out three thousand and thirty-seven ounces, worth $50,000, [gold was then $16 an ounce] from a strip four hundred feet along the creek by twelve feet wide. In no place did his excavation to bed-rock exceed four feet, and usually but three. A Mr. Patterson and his brother brought back $10,000 as a result of five weeks' mining on Lowhee. Their largest day's return was seventy-three ounces, worth about $1,200. The gold on this creek was in rough, jagged pieces, sometimes weighing six or even ten ounces.

On Lightning Creek, Mr. Ball reported on October 1, 1861, that one Ned Campbell had taken out the almost fabulous sums of nine hundred ounces the first day, five hundred ounces the second day, and three hundred ounces the third day. Another authority says that this claim, which cost $25,000 to open, returned $100,000 in three months.

The returns from Antler Creek for 1861, while respectable, are far below such colossal figures as the above. One company of four men were making from four ounces to nine and one-fourth ounces each per day; and the ordinary yield was from $20 to $50 per day for each man employed. The Reverend R.C. Lundin Brown records his being present when $1,000 were taken out of the sluice boxes as the result of one day's work.

On Keithley Creek, in 1861, the returns were smaller. Several companies were making from $50 to $100 per day to the man in the bed of the creek, and somewhat better in the bench diggings. Most of the miners were making from two ounces to three ounces per day. During this summer there were some two hundred men on the creek. Outside of the mining upon the creek itself, Keithley — the collection of houses at the mouth of the creek — was the supply centre for the Cariboo Lake and North Quesnel region.

So ends the year 1861. Taken all in all, a very successful year. Statistics give the output of gold for 1861 as $2,666,118. But behind this, and more important, was the general feeling that all the creeks of Cariboo were gold-bearing. To the outside world went reports of great "finds" — stories of men who in a season sprung from penury to wealth — exaggerated tales of rich deposits as wondrous as those that Ali Baba and Aladdin found.

Said the *Puget Sound Herald* : "The excitement respecting the Cariboo

The Aurora claim, above, was just downstream from Barkerville and yielded $850,000 with gold at $16 an ounce. (At the early 1980s price of gold this yield would have been worth over $40 million.) Miner Bill Phinney, below in 1868, washes tailings with a hand rocker at the Caledonia claim which yielded $750,000.

mines is fast reaching fever heat in this vicinity. People will not think of or talk about anything else, even the battles of the Rebellion are forgotten or cease to interest them, so engrossing is the subject of the new mines. Everybody talks of going to the Cariboo Diggings in the spring. We may, therefore, confidently look for a rush to these mines next season, equalled only by the Fraser River excitement of '58. So far as we can learn every miner from this new gold field has brought with him from $5,000 to $20,000, all of which has been obtained in the short space of two or three months."

Here was the genesis of the "rush" of 1862 — not from California alone, but from the Eastern States and the Canadas [essentially, today's Ontario, Quebec and the Maritimes], from the British Isles and the Continent. These immigrants came principally by the recognized route by way of Panama, San Francisco, Victoria, and thence up the Fraser. But as in 1858, so in 1862, when the end of navigation was reached miles of forbidding and dangerous land travel intervened. As the song ran:

"Five hundred miles to travel where naught but mosses grew
To cheer the weary traveller on the road to Cariboo."

The Gold Commissioner of Cariboo, in the fall of 1861, had "laid over" the claims until June 1, 1862; that is to say, he had suspended until that date the operation of the law which rendered a claim invalid if it remained unworked for seventy-two hours. This was necessary, as the mining then being confined to shallow diggings — from three to twelve feet in depth — it was impossible to carry it on during the rigorous winter of Cariboo. By the end of May probably six thousand miners had entered Cariboo, making their way under great difficulties, so as to be on the ground when the "lay over" should expire. Some had in three weeks walked the whole distance from Lillooet, carrying fifty- and sixty-pound packs. Over two thousand expectant men were on Williams Creek alone.

Thus was created an unprecedented demand for food and supplies, and these, becoming very scarce, commanded famine prices. For example, flour, bacon, beans, and salt were $1.50 a pound, dried apples $2.50 a pound, and gum-boots $42.50 a pair. The "lay over" period was extended to July 1st. This, with the high prices, disheartened many, who returned to the lower country. While some of the disappointed denounced the country as a humbug, the majority had faith in Cariboo, only complaining of being starved out. They were loud in their demand for a road to the mines so as to provide sufficient supplies at reasonable prices, declaring that wagons must be employed, as there were not enough mules in the colony to bring in over the miserable trails then existing the necessary food and implements.

On Williams Creek mining went on above the canyon, where the shallow diggings continued to pay well. Edward Stout had ventured to try the mouth of Stout's Gulch, which is below the canyon, and had there found, at comparatively shallow depth, the dark colored, water-worn gold of Williams Creek. Going deeper he found the bright, jagged, and more valuable Stout's Gulch gold. Encouraged by these results, William Barker, commonly called Billy Barker, had taken up a claim still further down Williams Creek, in the vicinity of the present town of Barkerville.

The other miners ridiculed this action, believing that all the gold was above the canyon; but he persevered and drew the prize of 1862. "Billy

Barker has struck the lead on Williams Creek on the flat below the canyon at a depth of fifty-two feet, obtaining $5 to the pan." A few days later the Canadian company was similarly fortunate. Then John A. Cameron, "Cariboo Cameron," found the lead even lower down the creek. Opinions changed. Below the canyon became the favorite spot. These deep diggings, from fifty to eighty feet, gave an air of permanency to Williams Creek, which contributed a large proportion of the $2,656,903 credited to the mines of the colony during 1862.

Lightning Creek, owing to the great expense attendant upon the opening of claims there, gave up a little of its treasure; still the greatest confidence was felt as to the ultimate result of operations thereon. Being most extensive, it was expected that, with the advent of cheaper supplies, it would contribute its full quota towards the general yield. In 1862 shafts were sunk from Eagle Creek to Davis Creek, along Lightning, but below Van Winkle they were uniformly unsuccessful, being unable to cope with the water.

Antler Creek was regarded as coquettish in 1862. Although on its banks good prospects were obtained and rich hill diggings announced, still the result was disappointing. One claim, Murray's, yielded in three days eighty-five ounces to each man employed; another, Hoy's, gave seventy-two ounces as the result of six men's work for half a day; while a third, Edward's, produced over $3,000 in a week. These were the best, and their returns were much above the average.

The year 1863 was the banner year of Cariboo. Williams Creek was mined along a stretch of seven miles, and about four thousand men found employment there. The deep diggings below the canyon were in full swing. Gold was being produced on a scale which exceeded California in its palmiest days. The results were in many cases almost incredible. A few isolated, well-authenticated instances will be given, because the reports of such golden harvests went abroad and aided to draw to the colony many persons filled with hopes of similar success.

The Cameron claim yielded, during 1863, from forty to one hundred and twelve ounces to each of three shifts per day. In October, John A. Cameron, "Cariboo Cameron," its principal shareholder, brought out about $150,000, his share of its yield for three months. Viscount Milton and Dr. W.B. Cheadle [Cariboo's first tourists. See page 58.] saw a wash-up on the Raby, which filled one of the tin cases used for preserved meats, holding nearly a quart and valued at about $5,000, the result of fifteen hours' work. Amongst this were several shillings and quarter dollars, which had dropped out of the men's pockets and turned up again in the dump box. The Diller took out one hundred and two pounds Troy in a single day. The Cunningham produced, on an average, $2,000 per day during the whole season.

The following summary shows the returns from the principal claims on Williams Creek to the end of 1863: The Adams yielded $50,000 from 100 feet; the Steele, $120,000 from 80 feet; the Diller, $240,000 from 50 feet; the Cunningham, $270,000 from 500 feet; the Burns, $140,000 from 80 feet; the Canadian, $180,000 from 120 feet; the Neversweat, $100,000 from 120 feet; the Moffatt, $90,000 from 50 feet; the Tinker, $120,000 from 140 feet; the Wattie, $130,000 from 100 feet; besides the Black Jack Tunnel, Barker, Baldhead, Abbott, Grier, Wilson, Beauregard, Raby, Cameron, Prince of Wales, and numbers of others of world-wide fame. Forty claims at least paid handsomely, and from about twenty was taken out steadily, every twenty-four hours, from seventy to four hundred ounces.

Besides Williams Creek, Keithley, Goose, Cunningham, Lightning, Jack of Clubs, Grouse, Chisholm, Sovereign, Fountain, Harvey, Nelson, Stevens, Showshoe, Last Chance, Anderson, California, Thistle, Sugar, Willow, McCallum, Tababoo, and Lowhee each drew a share of attention, and miners were at work upon them all.

The narrow gulch of Lowhee Creek for a while bade fair to equal Williams Creek, as indeed its early production already mentioned had promised. When the bed-rock was reached on the Cornish claim $4 to the pan was obtained, and for a considerable period between three hundred and four hundred ounces a day were taken from the Sage Miller claim.

On Lightning Creek, one company — the Butcher — working on a hill claim sixty feet above the bed of the stream, struck "pay" late in the fall of 1863, taking out two hundred ounces in one day. Another company was making forty ounces a day on this creek.

The practical completion of the Cariboo Road in 1863 greatly decreased the cost of living in that distant region.

From the changed conditions flowed a further result. In the winter of 1862-3 Cariboo was practically a deserted land. Some eighty miners, only, remained. But in the following winter some five hundred or six hundred miners stayed on Williams Creek. In their moss-chinked, mud-roofed log-huts, with their large, cheerful fireplaces, they spent the short days and long nights, developing a rude sort of social intercourse, and whiling away the monotony with conversation and cards. Some even worked a great part of the time, for during the winter of 1863-4 a few of the claims — the Cameron, Raby, and Caledonia, for instance, being deep diggings — carried on operations. But the majority of miners and mine-owners preferred to take advantage of the annual "lay-over" and spend their winters in the more genial climate and more attractive surroundings of Victoria and San Francisco.

Cariboo drew to itself not only miners but all the classes that naturally congregate where money is plentiful and easily obtained. Gamblers flocked like vultures to the spot. The authorities resolutely set their faces against this evil, but the vice was too deeply rooted to be completely eradicated. It merely went under cover and continued to flourish in private. An anomalous class of females, known as the hurdy-gurdy girls, made their appearance in Cariboo. They were mostly of German extraction. They frequented the saloons and drinking places and, for a money consideration, danced with all applicants. But, at the same time, their morals were above reproach.

The pay streak, as the auriferous stratum was called, consisted, on Williams Creek, of a blue clay about six feet thick, mixed with gravel and decomposed slate. Above the canyon this stratum lay quite close to the surface, but below that spot the covering was, generally speaking, from fifty to sixty feet. The deepest shaft in this vicinity was one hundred and thirty-four feet, but even then it did not reach the bed-rock. The prevailing theory was that this pay stratum was the bed of an old creek, which, carrying down

One of the most famous Cariboo gold rush photos was taken August 23, 1863, by C. Fulton. It shows the rich Cameron Company claim with John A. "Cariboo" Cameron holding the gold pan. His share was some $350,000 but the money brought only grief. His wife died in Barkerville, their infant daughter had previously died in Victoria, and he mismanaged his money. He died destitute and is buried at Barkerville.

the drift gold, had allowed it to settle either on the bed-rock or in the blue clay above it. The debris of centuries then covered the treasure. Great changes in the earth's surface took place. Here a slide, there a convulsion, upheaving a portion and distorting another. The present bed of a stream was thus no index to its old and gold-bearing bed.

Here was the element of chance — the reason why a claim on a hillside was rich, while one right in the present bed was barren. One miner might be making $1,000 a day, while his neighbor above or below him found his claim worthless. The former had struck the old bed, the latter not. It is evident that such a condition was one for capital and cooperation to cope with. The individual miner could not take the risk, even if he had the means, of sinking a shaft fifty or sixty feet in a country where wages and provisions were so expensive. Deep diggings were not for him. Hence the Peace River excitement, the Kootenay, and Big Bend rushes of 1864 and 1865.

The yield of 1863 — the golden year of Cariboo — is officially given as $3,913,563, though Allan Francis, the representative of the United States, estimated it at about $6,000,000.

During 1864, the claims below the canyon on Williams Creek were all being worked and all paid in varying measures of success. The Wake-up-Jake, reaching bed-rock in this year, gave fifty-two ounces, equal to about $800, from one panful of dirt. The Ericson on Conklin Gulch, a branch of Williams Creek, which was opened in 1863, now produced a weekly return of one thousand, four hundred ounces. The Cameron claim continued to pay eighty to ninety ounces a day. In the fall, the Prairie Flower, earlier

known by a far less euphonious name, struck the pay, taking out in one day one hundred and seventy ounces.

A short distance below the Cameron claim, near a spot called Marysville, Williams Creek widens into a flat, locally known as the meadows. An effort was made to work this ground in 1864. The great difficulty below the canyon, and especially in this section, was to cope with the flow of water. As soon as the Cariboo Road came into being, improved steam pumps replaced the picturesque wooden water wheels which drove the home-made pumps. But while these were sufficient in the deep ground near Camerontown and Barkerville, they were of little service in the meadows.

An artesian mining company which had obtained a twenty-year lease of a half mile square in this locality undertook a different style of work. Instead of the old-fashioned shafts this company operated by means of an artesian well auger, bringing up a panful of dirt at each raise. For a short time they obtained good returns, the first day's washing giving one hundred and fifty ounces, but the scheme ended in failure. The regular style of mining was also tried on the meadows on a very extensive scale over a distance of about three miles, but without success, for want of adequate machinery and pumps.

The Tiger, Beaver, Richfield, and John Bull were among the claims on the meadows which never reached bed-rock, "never bottomed," as the expression was. From the claims immediately adjoining and nearer Camerontown a small amount was obtained, but the water could not be overcome. The Marysville, Phelan, and Hart, which lay within a few hundred feet, yielded $250,000 and $300,000 each. But in these instances the pumps controlled the water.

The opinion was, therefore, always strong that the meadows would yield enormously if the water could be kept out of the workings. But neither in 1864 and 1865, nor in the days of the Lane and Kurtz Cariboo Mining Company in 1870 and 1873, could it be got under control. That company, which had a lease of a portion of this ground, did succeed, by sinking a shaft in rock to a depth of one hundred and twenty-five feet and drifting one hundred and forty-five feet under the meadows toward the old channel, in getting a prospect of $25. But just as the golden result appeared at hand the water "slumgullion," as it was called, compelled a suspension. It was thought, in 1876, that a bed-rock flume from Valley Creek, two and one-half miles in length, might solve the riddle, but nothing was done, and the riches of the meadows, if they exist, defied the ingenuity of man.

Following the experiment of 1863, a considerable number of claims worked through the winter of 1864. Amongst them were the Oram, Adams, Elliott, Prince of Wales, Cameron, Moffatt, New York, Grizzly, Caledonia, Cariboo, Watson, and Canadian. This activity gave stability and an air of permanent settlement to the Cariboo region. Of the one thousand, five hundred miners, about seven hundred or eight hundred spent the winter there.

A word or two about the other creeks will suffice. On Cunningham Creek, in 1864, shallow diggings at eight to ten feet were struck. One company was taking out one hundred ounces a day with four men. In a short time four hundred miners had rushed to this creek, the majority of whom were making two to three ounces a day. On Lightning Creek, the Ayrshire Lass was producing from twenty-five to forty ounces a day, and five or six other claims were paying well. The Butcher claim took out $5,300 in three days and had the honour of producing the largest nugget found in Cariboo, thirty and one-sixteenth ounces. Lowhee Creek continued to produce regularly, but no striking returns were obtained.

The following statistics, taken from Harnett's Lectures, will give an idea of cost and returns from some of the principal mines on Williams Creek: The Cunningham claim, located in 1861, with four interests, cost $100,000 to work, and yielded, up to 1865, $500,000. The California, located at the same time, cost $150,000 to work and yielded during the same period $500,000. The Black Jack, located in 1862, with six interests, returned in two years $200,000, under a total outlay of $50,000 for work at $16 a day. The Tontine, located in 1861, with four interests, cost up to 1865 $100,000 for development and working, and yielded $500,000. The Dietz paid good wages steadily. All these were in the shallow ground above the canyon. Below the canyon the High-Low-Jack, with five interests, paid in June 1867, $12,000 to the share. The Alturas, on Stouts gulch, located in 1864, with eight interests, paid off in five weeks during 1866 an indebtedness of $23,000. Its complete output was $275,000. The Taff Vale, on the same gulch, cost $30,000 to open, and yielded from one hundred to two hundred ounces per week, giving a grand total of $300,000.

In closing our remarks upon the golden era of Cariboo it is fitting to add a few words about the miners themselves.

Reference has been already made to the death of John Rose. As this man was one of the most successful and energetic prospectors, a few details are given. The miners believed in his star and confidently expected that he could and would find diggings as rich as Antler and Williams Creeks. Thus his movements were the subject of careful investigation. In the spring of 1863 he set out from Williams Creek on a prospecting trip into the Bear River country. From that time no white man ever saw John Rose alive. His remains were never found, nor was any authentic information as to his end ever obtained. In Milton and Cheadle's *Northwest Passage by Land* it is stated that later in the summer there was found, hanging to a branch, a tin cup bearing the words, "Dying of starvation," thus indicating his end. But this is an error. The authors have confused the death of Rose with that of Donald Munro. That unfortunate man wandered into the same locality and was lost.

In June 1863, a miner, Sim Shiveley, while returning from a prospecting tour, stopped on Bear River, about one hundred and sixty miles from Richfield, to cook his dinner. Wandering along its bank he noticed a cloth hanging to a tree. His curiosity being aroused, he hastened to the spot and found there the gruesome remains of a man. At his head was a tin cup bearing these words: "Donald Munro, in the woods, lost June, 1863, is from Inverness Town, Scotland, born June, 1825." Not an ounce of food was found near the body. But the stripped bark of the neighboring trees spoke eloquently of his desperate efforts to sustain life. Rolling the dead man in his blankets, Shiveley buried him there.

Of all the miners of the early days in Cariboo none is more widely known than John A. Cameron. This man's spectacular rise to wealth entitled him to the sobriquet he bore — "Cariboo Cameron." Returning to Glengarry, Canada, [today's Ontario], in the fall of 1863, he purchased a farm of two hundred acres at Summers Town on the St. Lawrence and expended vast sums in improving it, but it proved a poor investment. He then purchased some steamboat stock and a sawmill and timber limits on Lake Superior. These, likewise, turned out badly. As a last desperate chance he staked the remainder of his money on a quartz mine in Nova Scotia. Still ill-fortune pursued him. He lost all. In 1888 he returned to Cariboo to make another fortune. In vain. He died there on November 7, 1888, aged sixty-eight years. His body, most fittingly, rests in the quiet little cemetery at Camerontown on Williams Creek, overlooking the scene of his unparalleled success.

As an example of the difficulties of transportation before the advent of the Cariboo wagon road, the following incident is reproduced. It will serve to cast a light upon the nature of the men of '62.

Early in October 1862, Mr. Moses Cross Ireland, with some others, were returning from Cariboo across Bald Mountain. They had reached within a short distance of a well-known landmark in that desolate district called the "colored man's house" when the snow fell so thickly that they could not see an object ahead of them. They lost the trail and, travelling about for some four miles, came on another party lost like themselves. Shortly afterwards they were joined by another man, Frank Fulford, a packer. He informed them that about half a mile farther on were a number

Billy Barker, opposite, is probably the best known of all Cariboo miners since the community of Barkerville is named after him. Although his share from the rich Barker claim was some $100,000, he died penniless.

Barkerville is today an historic park which hosts about 200,000 visitors a year.

of people, including Mrs. Webster and her two daughters, Mrs. Cusheon, and a girl of fourteen.

After a debate with his companions on the situation, no two agreeing, Mr. Ireland struck out in the direction where he thought the lost trail lay. Upon his taking the resolution six others decided to join him. They wandered about until night-fall without satisfaction and were preparing to camp for the night, when the welcome sound of a gun report attracted their attention and they made for the place they judged it came from. Soon they were rejoicing in the colored man's cabin where they remained for the night.

Early next morning they found the snow was four feet deep, but with three others Mr. Ireland started to rescue the party lost in the snow, some thirty in number. On reaching a high point on the mountain they encountered so much snow that they were obliged to return. Rigging up some kind of snow shoes they again started on their mission of mercy and discovered the lost party about sundown.

They were camped in a ravine cowering round a fire with some blankets rigged up to break the piercing cold wind that howled through the forest. Men, women, and children, with some surviving animals, were huddled together in a wretched state, their teeth chattering and eyes swollen by the smoke driven in all directions by the icy blast. They had been fasting for sixty hours and eagerly welcomed the provisions the rescue party had brought with them. They told Mr. Ireland that Frank Fulford and another man had left them to search for provisions.

Mr. Ireland saw from the deplorable straits the people were in that considerable assistance would be necessary to get them out of their perilous position on account of the depth of the snow. Leaving his companions with them he started out for help, hallooing as he went in case other benighted travelers might be within hearing and be attracted. One of his calls was answered from a canyon about half way back, to which he proceeded and there he found Fulford and his comrade.

They had struggled through the snow all day and at length, overcome by hunger, fatigue and cold, had given up all hope. Mr. Ireland supplied them with some food. Invigorated with that, and the confidence imparted by the presence of their deliverer, they crawled over the snow on their hands and knees for about a mile, where they reached the summit of the ridge. Here they traveled more easily down hill to the colored man's cabin, where they arrived about 9 o'clock that night.

When Mr. Ireland reported the miserable condition of the unfortunates he had left, about twenty men volunteered to accompany him to the rescue. Next morning they began their toilsome journey as soon as they could see daylight. Breaking a trail through the deep snow, they succeeded in getting the whole party, including the surviving animals, back to that haven of rest, the colored man's cabin, in safety. Mrs. Webster was placed upon the stoutest animal and the youngest daughter was occasionally carried by Mr. Ireland.

Thus were a party of thirty persons providentially rescued, mainly through the perseverance, courage and foresight of a heroic gentleman, Mr. Ireland. He was overwhelmed with the grateful thanks of the rescued party, who clamorously insisted upon bestowing pecuniary rewards upon their rescuer, which he as persistently declined.

Roads and Trails to the Goldfields

When the miners arrived in 1858 the trails leading from the lower Fraser region were only the abandoned trail of the Hudson's Bay Company from Fort Kamloops to Fort Yale, and the existing trail from Fort Kamloops to Fort Hope. These routes were of comparatively small value to persons wishing to ascend the Fraser. Moreover, owing to their elevation, they were snowbound about eight months of the year. But there existed then, as there had existed from the earliest times of which we have any record, Indian trails along the banks of the river — trails of which Simon Fraser has left such a vivid description.

To get supplies into the region beyond Yale and to reach the mining bars above the canyons were the problems of 1858. The raging torrent closed

the river; the approach must be by land. The "almost insurmountable barrier" which the country beyond Yale presented caused Governor Douglas to give his attention to a route by way of the chain of lakes from Harrison Lake to the Fraser at Lillooet. This line of communication had been long known to the Hudson's Bay Company and had been mapped by Mr. A.C. Anderson, one of their chief traders. The fact that only short bits of trail were necessary to connect the stretches of water appealed strongly to

James Douglas, opposite, Governor of the Crown Colony of British Columbia.

Bottom: Chief Trader A.C. Anderson who discovered and mapped a route around the treacherous Fraser Canyon, below.

Douglas. The question he had to solve, however, was how to build these bits, short as they were, with very limited funds.

Late in July 1858, he invited the miners then in Victoria to consider the undertaking. The arrangement ultimately made was unique. Five hundred miners, divided into twenty companies of twenty-five men each under the command of a captain, were to be given free transportation from Victoria to the point where the trail was to commence, and to be supplied free with food during its construction. They were to receive no remuneration for their labour in building the trail. Each miner was to deposit $25 as security for the fulfilment of his agreement, which sum was to be repaid in provisions at Victoria prices when the work was completed, together with a fair allowance to cover the carriage of such provisions to the end of the trail.

The first detachment, two hundred and fifty men, left Victoria in the *Otter* on August 5, 1858; the remainder followed on the 10th. Their first act was to name the western terminus of the trail Port Douglas, in honour of the Governor. At the outset the work progressed rapidly. Ten miles were built during the first four days, and when the whole body was at work, from four to six miles daily. But the transportation of materials and supplies became more serious with the increasing distance. It was supposed that mules would be put on the finished trail for this purpose, and thus it was expected that the work would be completed in four or five weeks. Some delay and considerable dissatisfaction arose over the failure to supply these animals promptly, for in the interval all supplies had to be carried by the men themselves.

The trail was completed about the end of September. It was not a mere mule trail, but was well built, with bridges at all necessary points, and almost sufficiently wide for wagon use. Its entire length, including the lakes, was about one hundred miles. As completed, goods could be packed over it for 20 cents a pound. Some difficulty occurred in arranging the amount to be allowed for the transportation of the road-makers' supplies from Douglas to Lillooet. The men thought that 20 cents a pound should be allowed, while the representative of the Government would allow but 4 cents. When the question came before the Governor himself, he directed that the promised supplies be either transported over the trail to Fraser River at the Colony's expense, or a fair allowance, which he fixed at 18 cents a pound, be made to the men.

This trail gave ready access to the Fraser at Lillooet, reducing, consequently, the cost of food on the bars in that vicinity. At this time the charge for packing from Fort Yale to the Forks [Lytton] was 46½ cents, while from Douglas to Lillooet — almost double the distance — it was, by this work, reduced to 18 cents a pound.

But the gradual advance from Yale had shown the auriferous nature of all the bars between that point and Lytton. Hence, while the trail to Lillooet afforded access to the upper Couteau [Thompson] and Canoe countries, it gave no relief for the territory between Yale and Lytton. The Hudson's Bay Company's Brigade trail, as far as Spuzzum and Anderson River, and the Indian trails, were the lines of communication. In August, Douglas called for proposals to cut a mule trail from Yale by way of Douglas Portage to Spuzzum (sometimes called the Rancheria), and thence for a distance of thirty-five miles along the river. It was to be a trail over which a mule could pack two hundred and fifty pounds.

While this proposal was under consideration, a company of one hundred and sixty men and four hundred mules and horses, in command of David McLaughlin, arrived at Lytton. They had made their rendezvous at Walla Walla. Learning from Mr. Wolfe, a trader of Fort Colville who joined them with a band of cattle, that the Indians were hostile, the party adopted a semi-military organization. Four divisions were formed and placed under the command of James McLaughlin, Hambright, Wilson, and Tucker. A German who lagged behind while crossing the Columbia Plains was taken by the Indians and murdered. Near the boundary line, and on the east side of the Okanagan River, the party met the Indians in force and strongly entrenched. When the latter fired, the whites took shelter behind the rocks and returned the fire. All the afternoon the battle continued. Hurley, Evans, and Rice — three Californians — were killed, and six others wounded. Five horses were also lost in the conflict. During the night the Indians set fire to the grass to burn out the whites, but the latter set counter fires, and both held their positions. In the morning the savages had decamped. From the breastworks which they had erected it was evident that about a hundred Indians had been engaged in the encounter.

A few days later a large band rode down upon the party and endeavored to stampede their animals. Failing in the attempt, peace was made. No sooner had this been arranged than the Indians stole about sixty of Mr. Wolfe's cattle. McLaughlin's men, finding them in the act of jerking the beef, took them prisoners and were about to execute speedy justice upon them when Chief Trader Allen McDonald of Fort Colville most opportunely arrived on the scene. At his intercession the malefactors were released.

The whole journey occupied about thirty days. The trail was described as being so bad that one, who had once travelled it, would not desire to do so again.

Immediately after their arrival, one hundred of the mules were sent down the river trail towards Yale. When this news reached Yale, a meeting of the miners was held and about a hundred men volunteered to render the trail by way of Spuzzum and Boston Bar.

They set to work and made the trail as far as Spuzzum so passable that a mule could travel it with a load of two hundred pounds. The Governor took up the work where these volunteers ceased.

From Fort Yale to the Ferry the trail was in fair condition, but the remainder of the distance to Lytton was very rough, full of big logs and difficult places to travel, though loaded mules managed to pass over. By September 7th it was estimated that five hundred mules were packing over this trail from Yale to Lytton.

Besides this trail, there were two others known as the "Lower" and "Upper" Canyon Trails. The former was a rough path carried along a ledge of boulders at the bottom of the canyon, but openly passable when the water was low. The Upper Trail passed from ledge to ledge at a height varying from fifty to eight hundred feet above the river. They connected with the mule trail and afforded short cuts to those whose nerves were strong enough to stand the strain. The test came in rounding the cliffs.

The lower trail through the Fraser Canyon was passable only in early spring and autumn. At other times the trail was above the river, with often a straight drop of several hundred feet into the rapids.

Until completion of the Cariboo Wagon Road mules were the main method of packing supplies 400 miles to the Cariboo. A mule train travelled about 15 miles a day, a round trip to the mines taking about two months.

Here the Indians had suspended poles by ropes of deer hide and fibre, and in passing there was nothing for the traveller to grasp. He could only stretch out his arms and clasp the face of the rock, keeping as close to it as possible. If he became dizzy, or made a false step, the pole would swing away and place him in danger of toppling off. Yet the Indians who were accustomed to the work used these two trails for packing in supplies for the miners when the mule trail, owing to its elevation, was blocked with snow. The miners themselves were also obliged to use the same routes, dangerous as they were, and to carry their provisions along this hazardous pathway during a great portion of the year.

Judge Begbie passed over these trails in the following April. He describes them as being: "Utterly impassable for any animal but a man, a goat, or a dog." He adds: "It might, doubtless, be very much improved. In many places a very painful and dangerous ascent and descent of twenty minutes, in the whole course of which the traveller depends almost as much on his hands as on his feet, brings the path to within a few yards of the projecting precipice, through which a few pounds of powder would have made an easy way."

Lieutenant Mayne had no better opinion of these trails through the canyons: "The ground over which the trail passes is the roughest on which I have ever travelled, the greater part of it being over sharp-pointed rocks or granite boulders. Some of the ascents in the Great Canyon, which is six miles long, are from 30° to 60° and nearly perpendicular over the water."

In 1860, the Governor entered upon his road construction policy. He had realized from the beginning that roads were a prime necessity. But mining is proverbially uncertain, and the unstable mining community, rushing hither and thither as reports of rich strikes reached them, kept in doubt the proper line of permanent roadway. However, it was plain that access to the Interior must be given. The first step was to transform the existing trail from Douglas to Lillooet into a wagon road. After Lieutenant Palmer had examined it in May 1859, about a hundred men of the Royal Engineers were employed in improving the portion near Douglas.

In March 1860, Captain Grant, R.E., with eighty men of the corps, spent some time endeavoring to deepen the channel through the shoal of Harrison River so as to allow uninterrupted navigation at all stages of the water as far as Douglas. Later this party resumed work on the road. By October, with the assistance of some civilians, they completed it from Douglas to the Twenty-eight Mile House at Little Lillooet Lake in such a manner as to receive the highest encomiums from the Governor. A number of freight wagons were placed on this section, and thus the cost of transportation was again reduced.

In the following year the Royal Engineers continued their work on the same portion, reducing the grades and improving the roadbed. When it was completed Lieutenant Mayne described it as "a wagon road which would be no discredit to many parts of England."

The contract for the Douglas-Lillooet road on the second portage — Lillooet Lake to Anderson Lake, a distance of twenty-four miles — was in August 1861 awarded to Colquhoun & Company. This was to be eighteen feet in width instead of twelve feet. The contractors were unable to complete the undertaking beyond the first eight miles. In August 1861, the contract for finishing it was awarded to Joseph W. Trutch. In October 1861, he had one hundred and fifty men at work and was pressing construction rapidly forward. Between Anderson and Seton Lakes — one and one-half miles — Mr. P. Smith had a tramway in operation by the fall of 1861. From Seton Lake to Lillooet — four miles — the road was built by Mr. Watson and completed by November 1, 1861.

With the opening of navigation in 1862, freight wagons and stages were in operation over the whole extent of the Douglas-Lillooet route. Steamers were plying on the various lakes — the *Marzella* on Lillooet Lake, the *Lady of the Lake* on Anderson Lake, and the *Champion* on Seton Lake.

Taking the hint which the Gold Commissioner at Yale had thrown out, the Governor determined to build a trail along the mountain side from Fort Yale to Spuzzum, and from that point to Boston Bar, following the course of the Fraser at a moderate elevation. As already stated, the Brigade Trail could only be used during about four months in the year. In June 1860, a contract was made with Franklin Way of Spuzzum and Josiah C. Beedy of Yale, to build this trail, as far as Spuzzum. Messrs. Powers and McRoberts, in the same summer, built the trail from Spuzzum to Boston Bar at the mouth of Anderson River. When the Governor made a tour of the colony in October 1860, the trail was completed and open for traffic. "In riding over the face of these frowning cliffs, which a twelve month ago seemed to defy all efforts at improvement, it was impossible to suppress a feeling of thankfulnes and intense gratification at the successful issue of our labours and their probable influence on the trade and development of the country. The arduous part of this undertaking — excavating the mountain near Yale — was executed entirely by a detachment of Royal Engineers under Sergeant-Major George Cann, and it has been completed in a manner highly creditable to themselves and to the officers who directed the operation."

[Tolls were placed on the new trails in October 1860. The charge was 25 cents for every fifty pounds. Miners' packs not exceeding thirty pounds and goods that were the property of Indians were exempt from charges. Despite the tolls, the new trails were an immediate success and soon long lines of mules were carefully picking their way along the precipitous slopes of the Fraser Canyon northward to the mines of Cariboo.]

The mule trains usually consisted of from sixteen to forty-eight animals. No pack saddles were used. Instead a rough sort of leather sack, filled with straw and called an "aparajoe," was girded tightly upon the mule's back. Upon this was lashed the freight (two hundred and fifty or even four hundred pounds), and secured with the celebrated diamond hitch. A bell animal, usually a white mare, led the train. There was no control over the mules when packing, though each knew its place.

Besides a cook and a superintendent, or cargodore, there was a crew, as they were called, consisting of one man for every eight animals. The packers first followed the Brigade Trail from Yale to the crossing of Anderson River, made their way down that river to Boston Bar, thence took an Indian trail over Jackass Mountain to Lytton. When Powers and McRoberts built the trail from Spuzzum to Boston Bar along the left bank of the Fraser, the packers took that route instead of the Brigade Trail. In detail the route was, 1st day, Yale to Spuzzum; 2nd day, Spuzzum to Lake House; 3rd day, Lake House to Thousand Dollar Bill on the top of the hill from Boston Bar; 4th day, Thousand Dollar Bill to Butcher Flat; 5th day, Butcher Flat to Boothroyd Flat; 6th day, Boothroyd Flat to Kanaka Bar; 7th day, Kanaka Bar to Lytton; 8th day, Lytton to Nicomen; 9th day, Nicomen to Cook's Ferry. Four miles beyond Cook's Ferry the Thompson was left and the remainder of the route to Quesnel Forks was made in seventeen or eighteen days. The rate of travel there was about fifteen miles a day.

On this part of the journey there were no regular day's travel; the camping places depended upon water and feed for the train. The trip upward occupied about a month; the return a little less. Three trips were made in a season. Nevertheless, packing was the most lucrative of employments. The train soon paid the capital expense, and then great profits were made. Early in 1861 the rate from Yale to the Forks of Quesnel was $1 a pound. From that point to Antler, before the trail was made, Indians packed for 40 cents a pound. The rate fell as soon as pack trains could reach Antler Creek. In the summer of 1861 the charge for packing from Yale to Quesnel Forks had fallen to 40 cents a pound. In July 1861, four hundred and eight pack animals left Yale for the Cariboo mines.

Besides the mule trains, there was introduced into the colony in 1862 another pack animal, a stranger to our climate, the camel. Mr. Frank Laumeister, a prominent merchant and packer, was the originator of the scheme. It was thought that an animal that could subsist on sage brush, carry a thousand pounds, travel thirty or forty miles a day and go from six to ten days without water would be a success. Camels had been used in 1857-8 by the United States government in connection with the army transport service in Texas and Lower California. With this knowledge Mr. Laumeister procured a band of twenty-one.

They arrived in May 1862, and were at once sent to Douglas to pack on the portages, as the Douglas-Lillooet road was called. Though they could easily carry twice the load of a mule and pick their own forage, they were not entirely satisfactory. The rough, rocky trails with intervals of marsh and muddy ground were unsuitable for animals whose feet were accustomed to sand. Yet they remained in the business of packing for over a year and made regular trips to Cariboo. They were a great annoyance to the mules on the trail; the latter became quite unmanageable when they scented the strange beasts. Several accidents occurred in consequence, litigation arose, and the owners deemed it the part of wisdom to withdraw them from the road. Some of them were brought to the coast and disposed of, but the remainder were taken over to the Thompson River and turned out to spend their declining days far from their Arabian homes. For years they were a source of terror to horses and mules in the vicinity. The last survivor died about 1905.

How the Cariboo Road was Built

In October 1861 Governor Douglas, while at Yale, discussed the feasibility of constructing a wagon road along the Fraser to Lytton and thence to Cook's Ferry on the Thompson. The trail built the preceding year to Spuzzum pointed the way. The Governor was much impressed with the plan. Before departing he arranged to let the contract for the portion from Boston Bar to Lytton, a piece of comparatively easy work, with the exception of the part over Jackass Mountain, and ordered a party of the Royal Engineers to survey for a wagon road from Yale to Boston Bar and from Lytton to Cook's Ferry. He also sent out Sergeant McColl with another party of Royal Engineers to select a site for a bridge over the Fraser. The scheme so launched — a bold and daring one for a colony of such limited means — meant the overthrow of nature's gigantic barriers. It meant the quarrying of a roadway eighteen feet wide through those immense shoulders of rock that buttress the Cascades for miles along the Fraser's canyons. To provide an easy means of access to Cariboo was, in Douglas's opinion, a paramount duty of Government. Although the labour was Herculean and the distance four

G. B. Wright built about one-half of the 400-mile-long Wagon Road. Mule teams at Jackass Mountain, steepest grade on the route.

The Wagon Road bridge at Spuzzum, completed in 1863 for $45,000, was Western Canada's first suspension bridge.

hundred miles, yet travel must be rendered easy, the cost of transportation reduced, and thereby the trade of miners secured and retained for the people of the colony.

About the end of October, Sergeant McColl recommended that the river be bridged at a point about one mile below Chapman's Bar, where its width does not exceed two hundred and fifty feet, and that the road be carried along the left bank, easy grades being obtainable (with the one exception of Nicaragua Slide) the whole distance to Boston Bar.

The surveys having been completed and the location of the suspension bridge settled, the work of construction went on apace along the greater part of the distance between Yale and Cook's Ferry. The first six miles were confided to the Royal Engineers. Captain Grant, R.E., with a party of fifty-three sappers, commenced this section in May 1862, and by the following November had completed a road which was described as "an enduring monument of engineering skill and patient toil." From the six-mile post (Pike's Riffle) to Chapman's Bar (Suspension Bridge), seven miles, the contract was in the name of Thomas Spence. The cost of this portion of the road was $47,000. From Chapman's Bar to Boston Bar, twelve miles, the contract was in the name of Joseph W. Trutch. Work on this section was commenced in May 1862. It was finished during the latter part of the year at a cost of $75,000. In April 1862, after six months' delay, the contract for the road between Boston Bar and Lytton, thirty-two miles, was awarded to Thomas Spence for $88,000.

By the end of June almost four hundred men were employed, and twelve miles had been completed. Though these three contracts were held in individual names, they were really for the benefit of the partnership of Spence and Trutch. In March 1862, tenders were asked for a wagon road eighteen feet wide — this was the width of the whole Cariboo Road — from Lytton, via the Nicomen River, to Cook's Ferry [Spence's Bridge], twenty-one miles along the line blazed by the Royal Engineers in the autumn of 1861, to be completed July 15, 1862.

Charles Oppenheimer and Walter Moberly secured the contract. With them was associated Thomas B. Lewis. In May they were advertising for one thousand men for this work. For a time all went well, and great vigour was shown in its prosecution. The first twelve miles were completed to the entire satisfaction of the Government in June 1862. The time for completion was extended and the formal contract signed on August 16, 1862. But the wild rumours of the untold riches of Cariboo made it extremely difficult for the contractors to obtain anything like the proper number of men. In this dilemma resort was had to Chinese and Indian workmen, but the virulent outbreak of smallpox in 1862 spread consternation and death amongst the latter, cutting off this source of supply.

On September 30th the Government gave notice that unless the number of workmen was increased to three hundred, and the work energetically pressed forward, the contract would be cancelled; and a fortnight later the threatened action was taken. The Government took possession of the finished road, the unfinished work, and all the contractor's tools and outfit to recoup itself for advances made, and later in the season completed the work. Mr. Moberly, one of the contractors, was in charge for the Government.

The Harrison-Lillooet Road, as completed in 1861, terminated on the Fraser River at Cayoosh [Lillooet]. Later in that year Gustavus Blin Wright, the most famous of all the road-builders of colonial days, built the forty-seven miles thence to Clinton, sometimes called Cut-off-Valley. On August 16, 1862, the formal contract was made with him covering the construction of a wagon road from Lillooet to Alexandria. The country through which this two hundred and forty-four miles of road was to pass offered but few obstacles.

In May 1862, Mr. Wright was advertising for five hundred men to work on this road, and by the end of July 1863, it was completed to Soda Creek. When finished a short time later, Billy Ballou, the pioneer expressman, declared: "It is a No. 1 road for any country." Thus the first traversable road to Cariboo, that by way of Lillooet, was in operation in the summer of 1863.

By June 1863, the road from Yale to Cook's Ferry had been completed, with the exception of about one mile in Mr. Trutch's contract between Chapman's Bar and Boston Bar. In that short space, however, were several rocky bluffs, necessitating heavy blasting operations and requiring some two or three months' work to overcome. Notwithstanding the unfinished state of the road, freight in large quantities was transported along it during the early part of 1863.

As far as the ferry at Spuzzum, large mule wagons were used; thence to Cariboo everything was packed on animals' backs. The Indians, who had found lucrative employment in packing upon their backs supplies for the miners, and had even held their own against the mule teams on the rough trails, found themselves unable to compete against the mule teams on the road. Already the price of packing from Yale to Richfield, Williams Creek, which had previously been about 90 cents a pound, had dropped to 50 cents a pound. It was confidently expected that on completion of the road and the advent of wagons, the price would fall to 25 cents. It fell below that figure. In May 1864, it was 15 to 18 cents a pound.

To complete the Yale-Cariboo wagon road there remained, in 1863, to be placed under contract: (1) the suspension bridge to replace the ferry at Spuzzum; (2) a connection between Cook's Ferry and the existing road by way of Harrison-Lillooet-Alexandria, which Mr. Wright had built during that summer; (3) Cook's Ferry must give place to a traffic bridge across the Thompson. The two first-mentioned works were undertaken and completed in 1863.

On February 2, 1863, an agreement was made whereby Joseph W. Trutch undertook to build a suspension bridge, to be called the Alexandra Bridge, across the Fraser at the point which had been selected by Sergeant McColl in October, 1861. This was the first bridge on the suspension principle in either colony [Vancouver's Island and British Columbia]. The span was over three hundred feet. In the following September the bridge was finished at a cost of about $45,000 and accepted on the examination and report of Lieutenant Palmer. A four-horse team with a load of three tons was driven over as a sort of test, but the deflection was inappreciable, not amounting to more than a quarter of an inch.

The gap between Cook's Ferry and Clinton on the Lillooet-Alexandria road was closed during the summer of 1863. The first nine miles of this portion were built by the Royal Engineers under Lieutenant Palmer. William Hood of Cache Creek performed the remainder of the work, fulfilling his undertaking by August 1863. It was claimed that Hood's road was the best in the colony.

The avidity with which the public grasped the new conditions may be inferred from the fact that in July 1863, before the completion, a traveler reported meeting, between Cook's Ferry and Yale, ten loaded wagons carrying four thousand pounds each and two hundred and fifty pack animals, many of which had four hundred pounds on their backs.

In February 1864, Thomas Spence undertook to build a bridge, known as Spence's Bridge, in the vicinity of Cook's Ferry. The freshet carried away a part of the piers and did considerable damage. When the water subsided the work was resumed and completed late in the fall. The erection of this bridge, which cost about $15,000, was the last link in the chain from Yale

to Alexandria. On the strength of the loss by the freshet, Mr. Spence applied to the Legislative Council, in 1868, and obtained an extension of his charter right to collect tolls for two and a half years.

Before passing away from this portion of the subject reference must be made to the terms on which the roads, both by way of Harrison-Lillooet and by Yale, were constructed. Those portions which were built by the Royal Engineers were directly paid for by the Government of the Colony; the remainder of the Harrison-Lillooet road, as far as Lillooet, was paid for in cash and bonds; the Yale-Cariboo road, as far as Clinton, was also paid for in cash and bonds; but tolls were payable to the contractors on the Alexandra Bridge, Spence's Bridge, and the whole road from Lillooet to Alexandria for varying periods of five and seven years.

From Alexandria to Quesnel mouth the communication was for a long time by steamboat. The first vessel on this route was the *Enterprise,* built in 1863 by G.B. Wright at a cost of $75,000, the whole of the machinery

Opposite: The thin line across the cliff is the Cariboo Wagon Road. For miles the route hugged the Fraser River's rocky bank with Nicaragua Bluff, below, a typical section.

and boiler plates having been brought two hundred miles on the backs of mules.

Early in 1864 Wright undertook the construction of a wagon road from Quesnel to Cottonwood, on the way to Williams Creek, twenty-six miles. In July there were about one hundred whites and two hundred Chinese at work upon it. The former were mostly miners who had become disheartened with Cariboo and its deep diggings and were anxious to earn money to reach the coast or the Kootenay mines, where shallow diggings, the lodestar of the individual miner, were reported to exist. This portion was completed by September 1864, at a cost of about $85,000.

In 1864, F.J. Barnard put on a line of stagecoaches from Yale and Douglas to Soda Creek. The Cariboo Stage Company, Messrs. Humphrey, Poole, and Johnston, began in 1865 to operate stagecoaches on the newly-finished road from Quesnel to Cottonwood, connecting there with a saddle train for Williams Creek.

The remainder of the road from Cottonwood to Williams Creek was placed under contract in 1865. In June, Mr. Munro was given the contract as far as Barkerville for $45,000. Late in the fall this was completed and the last link in the chain was forged.

One of the results of the completion of the road was to reduce the freight to Cariboo from 75 cents to 15 cents a pound. But against this advantage the goods were subject to the tolls which have been specified. These levies were no inconsiderable sum, amounting often to more than the first cost of the merchandise. For example goods for Cariboo were subject to the tonnage tax of $3 per ton on leaving New Westminster; at Yale or Douglas a toll of 1 cent a pound was levied; on the Suspension Bridge a further charge of ⅓ cent per pound; on Spence's Bridge a similar charge; and another toll of 1 cent a pound on the road beyond Lytton and Lillooet — in all $56.33 a ton, or almost 3 cents a pound. When to this was added the freight rate of 15 or 18 cents a pound it will readily be seen that in many instances the cost of transportation doubled or trebled the price of the articles themselves. In 1865, the tolls collected amounted to $80,000; the cost of collection was $12,000.

Although somewhat out of chronological sequence, yet to complete the view of the Cariboo Road the attempt to utilize steam traction engines upon it for the transportation of freight may be mentioned. In 1864, R.C. Janion of Liverpool, W.L. Green of Honolulu, Henry Rhodes, and Joseph W. Trutch obtained permission to use these engines on the Cariboo Road. They were required to introduce three, at least, into the colony by May 1, 1866. The object aimed at was more speedy and cheap conveyance of supplies and material. The rights of the original promoters passed over to F.J. Barnard and J.C. Beedy.

Five of these engines and the necessary wagons were imported from Scotland, together with engineers to operate them. One was duly placed in commission and sent out from Yale with a load of twelve thousand pounds. It succeeded in reaching Spuzzum on the first day, Boston Bar on the second, and the top of Jackass Mountain on the third. There its journey toward Cariboo ended.

The rate of travel had been demonstrated to be no greater than that of the regular freight wagons. On the other hand, the cost was greater, owing to the enormous wear and tear, the expense of operation, and the necessity of strengthening all the bridges on the road. One of the engines was later employed in logging operations carried on by Jeremiah Rogers at Jericho on English Bay, and the remainder were returned to Scotland.

Reaching from Yale, the head of navigation, to the mines of Cariboo, a distance of nearly four hundred miles and solidly and substantially constructed by our infant colony in less than three years, this road was the pride of British Columbia. It was also a source of wonder and admiration to its visitors, who were loud in their expressions of surprise at the daring conception and skilful execution of the work. Here the road was supported by piling, there built upon immense masonry "fills," sometimes on gigantic crib-work, the ruins of which yet remain, sometimes cut through a sheer rock bluff, now almost at the water level, and anon raised to giddy elevations whence the river seemed but a silver ribbon.

As one writer noted: "If we could only look back into the past along that mighty highway, what a strange scene we should behold. Long lines of pack animals, heavy freight wagons, six-horse coaches, with the well-known faces of their passengers, camels and traction engines, an army of men with packstraps, some going, some returning, some successful, many unsuccessful, men drunk and men sober — all sorts and conditions of men — a motley crowd; bustling activity at the rough and ready roadhouses; such was the Cariboo road in the palmy days of its greatness that are no more."

With the completion of the Yale-Cariboo Road there were two conflicting routes to the mines — that which commenced at Douglas and that which commenced at Yale. From Clinton northward these two roads were merged. A great rivalry sprang up between them for the trade of Cariboo. The Douglas route being the older, had until 1863 a monopoly, or, at any rate, far the greater share of the business. The interested persons, the traders, the roadside house proprietors, the steamboat owners on the lakes, strove energetically to retain it. But natural conditions were unfavourable.

The difficulty in reaching even Douglas itself, owing to the shoals of the Harrison River, which necessitated transshipment except during the freshets; thereafter the constant changes from land to water travel, with the incidental delays in making connection with the steamers on the three lakes, soon settled the question in favor of Yale. On that route the freight was landed at all times of the year at Yale and, once placed in the wagons, could be sent through to the mines without any harassing delays. Against this was merely the extra toll on the Suspension Bridge and Spence's Bridge, which, together, only amounted to ⅔ of a cent a pound. From the completion of the road through the canyons, the Douglas route gradually fell into disuse.

The Chilcotin Massacre

Early in 1862 Alfred Waddington obtained a charter for the construction of the Bute Inlet Road, entitling his company to collect certain tolls for ten years on all merchandise carried over it. The surveying and preliminary work having been already finished, construction commenced immediately. By the end of April 1864, a road, or more properly a pack trail, had been completed for forty or fifty miles up the valley of the Homathco River. Sixteen white men in two parties, of twelve and four respectively, were at work four miles apart. Another man, Timothy Smith, was in charge of the ferry where the trail crossed the Homathco. Some sixteen Indians were also employed as packers to assist in the work. On April 29, 1864, three Indians came to the ferry, where a considerable quantity of provisions and supplies were stored, in charge of the ferryman.

They demanded food, which request being refused by Smith, they shot him. Then, fired with passion and possessed by the demon of blood, they hurried on ten miles further to the main camp of the road-makers. They reached it just before daylight. Their numbers were now increased. There twelve men unarmed, unguarded, thoughtless of danger, lay in the deep sleep of bodily exhaustion. The murderers surrounded the camp, cut the tent poles, and dropped the tents on their victims, firing into them with their muskets and using their knives until all but three were killed.

One of the survivors gave the following account of the massacre: "Proceeding inland from Bute Inlet, it was found necessary to engage a force

Judge Matthew Baillie Begbie, B.C.'s first judge, presided at the trial of the Chilcotin Indians. A fearless man who was knighted for his outstanding role in maintaining justice in a frontier land, he is commemorated by Mt. Begbie in the Cariboo.

The massacre trial was held at Quesnel, below in 1865. The Indians sentenced to death were hanged at the end of the street and buried in unmarked graves on the bank of the Fraser River.

of Chilcotin Indians to do the packing, etc. After a few days, sixteen Indians were engaged and they were followed by some squaws. At night all pitched tent and appeared satisfied. The evening previous to the massacre, the Indians put on war paint and had a sort of dance. Some of the whites did not like the appearance of things, yet nothing was said or done to the knowledge of the whites to cause suspicion of intended foul play.

"All retired as usual, the Indians camping, as was their custom, a few hundred yards distant. The whites lay three men in each tent and all was quiet, so far as the white men knew, up till about daylight, when the Indians commenced using their axes and striking right and left into the tents. We were awakened amidst groans and shouts, and some of our men trying to get up were either knocked down with axes or shot.

"A man was killed upon each side of me almost instantly. The pole of the tent fell lengthwise upon me and to this I attribute my escape. I kept still, and the Indians, thinking they had finished our tent, left; after all appeared quiet near me and, knowing what would be my fate if discovered when daylight broke, I quietly got up and started for the river near by. An alarm was given and shots fired at me, when I fell over a log at the edge of the river. I moved along the river bank for some distance.

"Apparently it was imagined that when I fell I had gone into the river. From where I was concealed I could see them throw the bodies of our men into the river. Some of the Indians packed up supplies at our camp.

"I soon left, and after going a few miles came across another of our party who had also escaped. Afterwards I met another, making three who had escaped, of the sixteen white men. When we got to Bute Inlet we got Indians to take us in canoes."

Indiscriminate plunder was not indulged in by the murderers. Money in considerable quantities lay scattered around. But all the food was taken. The tools and implements were left as the workmen had placed them, and were found in the same condition eight years later.

Four miles beyond this place the superintendent, Mr. Brewster, and three men were at work "blazing" the trail. Three of them were attacked and killed before resistance could be offered. The fourth, a half breed, endeavored to escape by running to the river, evidently intending to hide there or swim away. But the murderers' bullets overtook him near the bank, and the rushing torrent bore his body towards the others. The body of the superintendent was cruelly maltreated and abused. It was left where he fell.

The Indians, leaving the greater part of the booty concealed, then headed eastward into the Chilcotin. They appear to have received considerable reinforcements, amounting to about thirty in all, before they reached the house of a white settler, Manning, at Puntzi Lake. He was soon dispatched and the assassins, with continually swelling numbers, advanced to meet a pack train with eight drivers approaching from Bentinck Arm.

This train, in charge of Alexander McDonald, was carrying supplies for the Bute Inlet route, taking this means of avoiding the difficulties of that trail near the coast. Neglecting the warnings of McDougall's squaw, who had accidentally heard of the Bute Inlet murders, the party proceeded too far and, on attempting to retreat, were ambushed by the Indians, now fifty or sixty strong. Three of these men were killed, but the other five,

Alfred Waddington, whose road building project resulted in a massacre.
Top right: Chartres Brew, Chief Inspector of Police, led one group of volunteers.

two of whom were badly wounded, managed to escape. Amongst the killed was McDonald himself, who was last seen behind a tree taking aim with his revolver at Tellot, the chief, who had acted a prominent part in the destruction of Waddington's party. McDougall's squaw also fell a victim of the lust of blood. In all, nineteen persons were numbered in the death-roll.

Favoured by impunity the assassins now became promoted to the dignity of insurgents by the adhesion of the whole Chilcotin tribe from the summits of the Coast Mountains to the benches of the Fraser River. Fear spread over the whole Interior. It was reported that the Indians were combined for the purpose of killing every white man they met. The few settlers in the vicinity fled for their lives to the coast region.

Before proceeding to relate the steps taken by the Colonial Authorities to quell this outbreak, let us pause to ascertain its origin. There is no doubt that while the road-builders were well supplied with food, the Indian packers were nearly starved. That the desire for food was one factor is shown by the fact that all the food at the ferry was stolen and hidden away and all the food at the main camp taken. Revenge for wrongs, real or imaginary, was another.

These two items — plunder and revenge — form the basis. To them were added complaints that the whites — not those killed, but others — were obtaining the services of the Indians and giving worthless acknowledgements in payment. Other white men, it was claimed, had stolen from the graves of their dead the property left there. The great scourge of small-pox, which had made such ravages amongst the whole native population in 1862, was said to have been introduced amongst the Chilcotins by evil-disposed whites and revived later by unscrupulous white men who had removed from the graves the infected blankets and sold them to the unsuspecting natives. Further, that not content with this wicked conduct, some white men had threatened to bring the small-pox once more amongst them. That the desecration of their graves was regarded as a factor in the trouble is further shown by the fact that at the next session of the Legislative

Council an ordinance was introduced by the Attorney-General making such conduct an offense punishable by a fine of $500 and six months' imprisonment.

The news of the massacre of Waddington's road-builders reached the capital on May 14, 1864. Governor Seymour, who had arrived in the colony only a month before, found himself face to face with what threatened to develop into a general Indian uprising.

Immediate and energetic steps were taken. On Sunday, May 15th, a party of twenty-eight volunteers, under Chartres Brew, the Chief Inspector of Police, left the capital on H.M.S. *Forward* for the scene of action. Another party of fifty was organized in Cariboo, under the command of William G. Cox — "Judge Cox" — as he was commonly called. The Brew party was instructed to make its way into the Chilcotin territory by the Bute Inlet route, while the Cox party advancing from the eastward should effect a junction with it near Puntzi Lake. In the event of the Brew party coming into contact with the Indians before reaching that point, and meeting with resistance, the instructions were to return and report. Then H.M.S. *Tribune*, with an ample force of marines, would be dispatched as a reinforcement. The Brew party made its way to the end of trail but, finding no practicable road through the wild mountainous region which intervened between that point and the plateau, had to abandon the attempt to reach the Chilcotin. The party returned after a fortnight's absence.

The expedition from Alexandria under Mr. Cox did not set out for the Chilcotin until June 8th. The delay was caused by the steamer *Enterprise*, which operated from Quesnel southward, being out of repair, so that it was necessary to build rafts to reach Alexandria. This party consisted of fifty men, including Donald McLean, late Chief Trader of the Hudson's Bay Company at Kamloops, and two of his sons. From Alexandria Cox followed Lieutenant Palmer's trail of the preceding year and, on the 12th, arrived at Puntzi Lake near the junction of the Chilcotin and Chilanko Rivers.

The next day McLean departed for the forks of the Chusko and Chilcotin Rivers, through the thickly-timbered and brush-covered country, in search of Alexis, a friendly Chilcotin chief. When he reached this tribe he found all in arms and prepared for war. He succeeded, however, in convincing them of the peaceful intentions of the whites and they promised to send Alexis into the camp.

A scouting party was also sent out, but had scarcely proceeded half a mile when they fell into an ambush. One man was injured. The Indians dodged from tree to tree, whooping and firing upon the party at every opportunity. Their fire was vigorously answered. When this party returned to camp, the Indians came to the top of a hill near-by and fired their pieces in manifest token of defiance. Cox determined to await the arrival of reinforcements. In the meantime his party remained at Puntzi Lake in their log fort on the summit of a small hill from which flew continuously the white flag of friendship.

When the attempt to enter by way of Bute Inlet proved abortive, another party was dispatched on June 13th from New Westminster on H.M.S. *Sutlej*. Governor Seymour accompanied this contingent. The route selected was the Bentinck Arm Trail. When they arrived at the head of that arm on June 24th they met the five survivors of the McDonald party and thus learned the details of this late massacre. Visions of a general Indian war with all its horrible accompaniments arose. But when the Bella Coola were found to be most friendly and peaceful the fear of an insurrection, or even of a really organized resistance, began to disappear. Proceeding slowly inland the volunteers soon came upon the traces of the struggle of McDonald's men. Kegs of nails, boxes of carpenters' tools, looted packsaddles, broken agricultural implements, a musket shattered by a bullet, canned goods, ropes, candles, and all sorts of merchandise lay scattered around.

Farther on were the earth-works from which McDonald and his party had kept the savages at bay. Two miles beyond, on the summit of a hill near Sutliko, a palisaded blockhouse of the Indians was found. A clearing had been made around this spot and the building loop-holed for defence. As the works were capable of affording serious annoyance they were destroyed. Evidences of intention to oppose their advance were frequent, but the Indians fled before them in all directions. On July 7th the party reached Puntzi Lake, where Cox's men were anxiously awaiting their arrival.

McLean, who was in his element in this man-hunt and who seemed to think he bore an enchanted life, was indefatigable in his efforts to bring it to a successful issue. On July 17th he went out with an Indian guide to reconnoitre. The latter, hearing the click of a gun, warned McLean of the proximity of an enemy and advised him to lie down. He contemptuously spurned the advice. The next moment the sound of a gun was heard and McLean fell with a bullet through his heart. The guide, crawling through the woods, returned with the news and a party was sent out to bring in the body.

The force from New Westminster, hearing that the murderers were in hiding nearer the coast, set off in that direction, scouring the country and meeting, everywhere, evidences of the proximity of Indians, but finding none. Cox's party still remained in the camp.

By degrees the Indians, who had kept aloof at first, began to be familiar with the presence of this armed white force in their country. Women came to the camp to trade, and finally Alexis, the much-desired Chilcotin chief, was induced to present himself to the Governor. Accompanying him was an Indian who stated that he was the bearer of a message from Klattasine and Tellot, that if the whites would remain where they were the murderers would come and deliver themselves up.

Cox replied that he intended to proceed immediately in search of them and was only waiting for the necessary provisions from Alexandria, but if the murderers would surrender he would await for them at the old Hudson's Bay Company's fort on the Chusko River. On August 10th the messenger came, saying that eight of the murderers would arrive next morning. Accordingly, on the following day, Klattasine, Tellot, and six others accompanied by Alexis and a number of his people, came to Cox's camp and surrendered themselves. They returned at the same time a horse and a mule and $20 for the Governor in token of good faith, and bringing presents of money and gold dust. They informed him that ten others were implicated, but could not be caught until the following spring, and that

On a grassy knoll overlooking the Williams Lake-Bella Coola Highway at Mile 200 the trenches dug by Alexander McDonald and his men are still evident. At the site a Stop of Interest sign notes: "In 1864 Alexander McDonald and seven companions defended these earthworks against Chilcotin, Tatla and Sitlecee Indians. McDonald and two of his party were slain and four others wounded in the ensuing withdrawal toward Bella Coola."

Below: A photo taken in 1928 of the remains of the cabin where ferryman Tim Smith was murdered.

three more had been concerned in the murders but that one had been shot by McDonald and the other two had committed suicide.

The dramatic version of this incident runs thus: "The murderers sent one of their slaves to Mr. Cox's camp to ascertain the terms of surrender. Cox packed the slave with a sack of flour and other articles and sent a message to the effect that they desired to make friends with them and invited them into camp. About noon of the same day Tellot, with his party, accompanied by their families, came into camp, and found to their surprise that they were surrounded by armed men, who informed them that they were prisoners, and ordered them to lay down their arms. All, with the exception of Tellot, complied, but he grasped his musket by the muzzle and smashed it into atoms against a tree, and drawing his arms across his breast invited them to shoot him, remarking with scorn depicted on his countenance, that 'King George men were great liars'."

This story, unfortunately for its veracity, rests entirely upon a letter from William Byers, who was one of Brew's party and who, at the time of the surrender, was with them a hundred miles away. The account which has been given as the correct one is the official report of Mr. Cox, supported in detail by J.D.B. Ogilvy, an eye-witness.

There is, however, little doubt that while the theatrical gunbreaking incident is apocryphal, Cox made representations of friendship and immunity which he could not perform. This appears plain from the gifts which the Indians brought, and explains the otherwise unaccountable surrender of men whom the party had not even been able to see or get a trace of, and who could readily have hidden themselves securely in the fastnesses of the mountains. Chief Justice Begbie in his note on the subject says these men "were induced to surrender."

The ring-leaders having been secured, provisions being scarce, and the daily cost of the expedition enormous, Cox's party with the prisoners returned to Alexandria and disbanded. Brew's party marched to Bella Coola, hoping to find some of the other murderers on their way. In this quest they were unsuccessful, but meeting Anaheim, another chief of the Chilcotins, they obtained from him the horses and the greater part of the loot of McDonald's pack train. Not having been concerned in the massacres, though doubtless willing to aid the offenders, Anaheim was released, promising to secure the remainder of the fugitives in the spring and deliver them up to justice.

The trial of the murderers took place at Quesnel in September. Two of them became witnesses for the Crown; five were found guilty and hanged; the eighth was sentenced to imprisonment for life, but escaped. This outbreak killed the Bute Inlet scheme. No further work was ever done upon it.

[For almost a century the only access into the Chilcotin from the west was the packhorse trail from Bella Coola on which Alexander McDonald was ambushed and killed. In 1952, however, the citizens of Bella Coola grew tired of being promised a road and having nothing happen. They started the bold project themselves and on September 26, 1953, succeeded in pushing a road up and over the formidable Coast Mountains to create B.C.'s third route to tidewater.]

First Tourists to Cariboo—1863

INTRODUCTION:
Between 1858-1862 some 40,000 men from around the world were lured to the Fraser River and the Cariboo by the word "gold." All intended to become wealthy through finding nuggets by the pound or establishing hotels, saloons, stores, wayside stopping places and similar businesses. By contrast two men, Lord Milton and Dr. Walter B. Cheadle, had a startlingly different reason. They came "for pleasure" as Dr. Cheadle later wrote, thus becoming the first tourists to visit not only the Cariboo but also to cross Canada.

In the early 1860s, however, Canada was dramatically different from the 10 provinces of today. In the east was the province of Canada which comprised the Maritimes and a slice inland about one-third the size of Ontario and Quebec. In the west were two Crown Colonies, Vancouver's Island and British Columbia, both governed from England. In between was a massive region called Rupert's Land, the Stickeen Territory and the North-Western Territory. Bigger than Europe, it extended over 2,000 miles from east to west and 1,600 from the southern grassland to the Arctic Ocean.

Viscount Milton, far right, and Dr. Cheadle, centre, at San Francisco on their homeward journey in 1863.

Milton and Cheadle were two months fighting the wilderness from Jasper to Fort Kamloops and were lucky to survive. The sketch at left from their 1865 book shows their guide trying to rescue a packhorse from the Fraser River. A second horse drowned.

In the Cariboo they discovered that accommodation was frequently very basic, with up to 30 men sharing a room. The sketch below shows a roadhouse where they spent a night, with Cheadle noting: "The only bed was the floor ... at one end a large open chimney, and, at one side, a bar counter, behind which are shelves with rows of bottles containing the vilest of alcoholic drinks."

It was a massive fur preserve of the Hudson's Bay Company, their small isolated forts the only sign of white habitation.

Milton and Cheadle's journey from Atlantic to Pacific took them over a year. Luck was their companion, especially when they reached the Rockies. They were 6 weeks battling through 180 miles of wilderness between Mt. Robson and Fort Kamloops and almost died of starvation.

After they arrived back in England they recounted their adventures in a book, *North-West Passage by Land.* It quickly became one of the most popular travel books of the era, selling 8 printings, the 9th and final one appearing in 1891. Although both names appeared as authors, it was generally known that Cheadle had written the book and based it on his Journal of their venture.

For some 70 years the Journal was known mainly to Cheadle's heirs. Then in 1931 A.G. Doughty and Gustave Lactot of the Public Archives of Canada prepared the Journal for publication, calling it *Cheadle's Journal of a Trip across Canada 1862-63.* In the introduction they note:

"This is the journal of the first transcanadian tourist. Before him others either on business, exploration or duty, had crossed overland from Eastern Canada to British Columbia. But Walter Butler Cheadle was the first to traverse the whole country from the St. Lawrence to the Pacific simply 'for pleasure', for the sheer enjoyment of seeing new lands, hunting the buffalo and visiting the gold regions of Cariboo. He was then twenty-seven years of age, in the prime of his manhood, a sturdy son of Old England and a former Cambridge oarsman. This may explain his adventurous propensities, to which the reader is indebted for a faithful narrative of the primitive conditions and extraordinary hardships which attended a transcontinental trip through the mountainous solitudes of Western Canada — conditions and hardships which were faced with indomitable courage, and inexhaustible endurance. For one must remember that in 1862 the Prairie and Pacific provinces were really a wild West, a country without roads or settlements, and deserted with the exception of distant fur-trading posts and occasional roaming Indians.

"The author, Walter Butler Cheadle, with his companion, Lord Milton, left Liverpool in June 1862 and reached Quebec on the 2nd of July. By boat they proceeded at once to Toronto, visiting Niagara Falls, and then by railway through Detroit and Chicago to La Crosse, on the Mississippi. Here, they boarded a steamer which conveyed them to St. Paul, whence a journey by rail brought them to St. Anthony. From that place, they travelled by stage to Georgetown on the Red River. Here they took to the canoe and reached Fort Garry on the 7th of August.

"Soon the actual difficulties of the journey began. Equipping themselves with necessary food, arms and utensils, they purchased horses, secured reliable half-breed guides and left Fort Garry on August 23rd for the Prairies. Their first stop was at Fort Ellice on the Assiniboine and their next at Fort Carlton, on the North Saskatchewan, which they reached on the 26th of September.

"The season was now well advanced and therefore Cheadle and Milton went into winter quarters near White Fish Lake, at a place called Jolie or Belle Prairie, about eighty miles from Carlton, where they remained till the 3rd of April 1863. On that date, they returned to Carlton. Securing new guides and provisions they made preparations for the most difficult task of their journey, the crossing of the Rockies. Three days later, they started on their daring enterprise, stopping at Fort Pitt and later at Fort Edmonton, posts of the Hudson's Bay Company on the North Saskatchewan. On the 3rd of June, the party left Edmonton heading for the Rockies, having decided to cross the mountains by way of the Yellowhead Pass, at that time a very little known route.

"Here they faced an exceedingly arduous part of the trip. With a weak party and no experience of local mountain conditions, they reached Jasper House on June 29th and Yellowhead Pass, July 17th. Difficulties soon increased. Well-nigh impassable routes along the Thompson River owing to steep rocky hills, close forests and fallen timber, delayed their advance. A diminishing quantity of food, scarcity of game, the subsequent loss of provisions, instruments and horses, added to their hardships and privations, and reduced them to the necessity of killing their pack-horses to save the party from starvation. But thanks to an indomitable spirit and the resource of their French half-breed guide, they finally reached Kamloops on August 28th. But their condition was pitiable. Their clothes were in tatters, their faces were gaunt and haggard, and their bodies in a state of almost complete exhaustion from exposure, fatigue and lack of nourishment.

"At Kamloops the travellers re-victualled and proceeded to New Westminster and Victoria. Now they carried out the last part of their programme, by taking a trip by boat and stage to the gold regions of the Cariboo as far as Richfield...."

PUBLISHER'S NOTE: Milton and Cheadle arrived in Victoria on September 19, having taken over 14 months on their overland journey. They stayed in Victoria for 10 days then left by sternwheel steamer for New Westminster, beginning of their trip to the Cariboo. At New Westminster they attended a land sale where Milton, "carried away by the excitement," bought 7 lots ranging in size from 3 to 9 acres for from $100 to $160 each. Today the lots, part of downtown New Westminster, are worth many times more per foot than Milton paid for a 9-acre block.

On Thursday, October 1st, they boarded the sternwheel steamer Hope *for the first part of their journey up the Fraser River to Harrison Lake. During most of the night the sternwheeler "wooded up," or took on the 4-foot chunks of cordwood used for fuel. As Cheadle noted: "... but little sleep in our narrow berths, for which they charged us $2 each."*

On their upward journey they went via the Harrison-Lillooet route which bypassed the Fraser Canyon by a series of lakes and rivers. Late in 1858 a trail had been slashed around the Fraser Canyon to Lillooet and in 1860 it was widened to a wagon road. From Port Douglas on Harrison Lake the road led overland 38 miles to Lillooet Lake. Here a steamer, Lady of the Lake, *connected to a 30-mile road which led from Lillooet to Anderson Lake. Service on 19-mile-long Anderson Lake was provided by another sternwheeler, the* Marzelle. *From Anderson Lake 1½ miles of road led to 23-mile Seton Lake and another steamer, the* Champion . *From Seton Lake a road led 3 miles to Lillooet. Then in 1861 Gustavus Blin Wright began work on 47 miles of road from Lillooet to a point that became known as Clinton.*

But this route wasn't satisfactory. The road being built by Wright climbed over a 4,000-foot mountain and grades were steep and hazardous. From Port Douglas to Lillooet freight had to be transferred from steamer to wagon and wagon to steamer at least eight times, each transfer resulting in an increase in freight rates. It was evident that this route would never serve as the main thoroughfare to Cariboo.

Fortunately there were men of vision at the head of Government. In 1861 Governor Douglas outlined a plan as bold and imaginative as anything previously undertaken in North America. It called for construction of an 18-foot wagon road north 400 miles through the rock barrier of the Fraser Canyon and across the lonely wilderness miles to the goldfields. Considering that the permanent population of the colony was under 7,000, the project was a stupendous undertaking.

Work on the Cariboo Wagon Road began in October 1861 and by September 1863 had been completed from Yale in the Fraser Canyon 300 miles to Soda Creek in the Cariboo. The Harrison Lake-Lillooet route was soon abandoned. Milton and Cheadle, however, went to the Cariboo via the Lillooet route and returned on the new wagon road through the Fraser Canyon.

The following excerpt from Dr. Cheadle's Journal, *reprinted courtesy the Public Archives of Canada, relates the travellers' experiences during their 6-weeks trip to the Cariboo's golden creeks. Of the* Journal, *the Public Archives notes:*

"Written from day to day under all kinds of conditions it, naturally and fortunately, does not bother with style nor composition. But crammed with incidental details, it is a mine of interesting observations, accurate descriptions and vivid pen-pictures, interspersed with a rich vein of humour, simplicity and sportsmanship. It is a book that no lover of the West can ignore."

Friday, October 2nd—Going before daybreak, having anchored most of the night; a great flat boat full of hay lashed alongside & delaying our progress, so that we did not reach Douglas until 6 o'clock. 45 miles from New Westminster. Douglas [Harrison] Lake 45 miles long; immense numbers of salmon splashing about in shallows of rapid in Harrison River. Indian boys in canoes spearing them now in bad season. Bill on boat $10 each for 3 meals, passage & bed. Douglas a vile hole in hollow formed by continuation of lake basin up to hill beyond lake; put up at Macdonald's; wretched supper of pork & liver. Miners gambling & drinking. Yankees preponderating; scarcity of women. Silver mine on Harrison Lake; talk of working it.

Saturday, October 3rd—Find stage will not go till Monday. Walk up to inquire of Mr. Gaggin the Judge if there are any other means of getting forward. Regular jolly Irishman from Cork; kindly promises to lend Milton a horse if I can find another. Agree to start on horseback tomorrow. Introduced to a Captain Nunn, very stout & barefaced, small featured; & Dr. Sylvester a handsome young fellow with slightly grey hair & shaky hand.

New Westminster in the early 1860s with a sternwheel steamer at the wharf. The flat-bottomed vessels provided service to Victoria, Port Douglas and Yale.
The drawing below of Douglas appeared in the *London Illustrated News* in 1864. Here Milton and Cheadle began their overland trek to Cariboo.

Gaggin told us of miners & Chinamen coming down in canoes without their heads. [The Indians murdered scores of miners.] Barrett Lennard never came further than Harrison Lake into British Columbia, & Macdonald (another author) never beyond Langley. Delayed us with beer. About 5, stage came in with 10 miners. Prisoner brought in. Going up to see Gaggin, met a Sywash prisoner who had escaped, just recaptured, shot in the neck by constable altho' he did not resist; trotted along with string to the ring of his gyves [shackles].

Sunday, October 4th—After sundry beers & procrastinations we set out. Gaggin having found a mule for me for which I had to pay $10 for the 29 miles. The Judge accompanied us on a grey horse which had been left behind by a Mr. Flinn gone down to Victoria. "The Judge" turned out a "whale for drink," & we pulled up at every wayside house to refresh; as we started late our chance of getting thro' looked small; dined at the 10-mile house where we were so strongly advised by the Governor to have a feed; & a very nice clean dinner we had. Kept by a German named Perrin. From there we trotted on to the 16-mile house kept by an old Scotch ship's-carpenter named Waite, & finding it late, we resolved to stay the night & ride forward in time for the steamer in the morning. Gaggin & I had two jugs of mulled claret which made us sleep like tops.

Monday, October 5th—Off at 7 to catch the steamer at 12. At the 20-mile house there is a hot spring & baths; rude wooden affairs. Water a slight smell of sulphuretted hydrogen, & said by bath proprietor to contain common salt & nitrate of soda; reputation for cure of rheumatism; the water runs out of the solid rock at the foot of the hill in a small stream the size of one's finger; hot enough to boil an egg; similar spring at the foot of Harrison Lake. [The site of today's famous Harrison Hot Springs Resort.] My mule 'Yank' falling lame, I rode on, leaving Milton & Gaggin at the 24-mile house refreshing. Arrived at foot of the little lake (29-mile house) an hour before the steamer started, dined & waited in vain for Milton & Gaggin; the steamer at last starting & leaving us in the lurch; much annoyed at thus losing a day. Presently stage came in from Douglas, bringing only one passenger, Mr. Flinn whose horse Gaggin had impressed to ride along with us. Also "Hard Cussie" & another fellow of the well-known "Hard Cussie" claim. About 4 o'clock Milton & "The Judge" arrived, the latter having met some friends at the last house & gone through ½ doz. of stout!

Introduced to Mr. Flinn who has a farm & the ferry at Lillooet & kindly offered me his horse to ride over the portages. Gaggin & the landlady (an Irishwoman) had chaff all the evening; very nice clean beds. Country between Douglas & Little Lillooet Lake thickly wooded; very little farming country; flat patches of small extent; usual gorges & hills; mostly rocky ground.

Passed Summit Lake, water flowing in opposite directions supplying 2 rivers.

Tuesday, October 6th—Steamer brought in 2 prostitutes, white woman & negress, having spent the season in Cariboo (made fortunes). Over Little Lillooet Lake in tiny steamer, then portage past rapids (some ¼ mile) which are not passable at lower water; & then in fine steamer "Prince of Wales" over Great Lillooet Lake to Pemberton, a miserable rocky place. Gaggin accompanied us. Continual liquorings up, which Milton & I shirked as well as we could. Lakes surrounded with lofty rocky mountains sparsely wooded with pine & poplar. Arrived at dark.

Wednesday, October 7th—Bid a kind adieu to Gaggin, & then forward 24 miles to Anderson Lake; pretty good road & usual scenery; a little farming land called The Meadows 2 or 3 miles from Pemberton. Milton rode Gaggin's mare, & I Flinn's grey, both capital hackneys, & we went thro' at a great pace. Flinn borrowed a horse, & "Charley Chapman" the owner of the steamer, accompanied us. For dinner we stayed at the house halfway owned by a Virginian of the name of Ketterel. He had only been there a year. There is a fine open flat of I suppose 100 acres partly under cultivation, such good open land is rare. He bought at 2,000 dollars, & the first year's crops paid the purchase.... Ketterel was an ardent Southerner & the most gentlemanly American we have met, very quiet & does not "blow". He & Flinn praised the Governor highly, & assured us that, were there to be an election for the office, he would have 99% of the votes. Ketterel had two pretty little daughters whom he evidently idolized & the youngest who could hardly talk informed us lispingly that she was "for Jeff Davis", & when she went home she should "fight the Yankees". [The United States civil war in which 620,000 soldiers died was then raging.] Rode on rapidly to Anderson where we slept; Nice clean house kept by Frenchman; meals $1 each. Beds $1. Horses $1 per bed.

Thursday, October 8th—Away at 6.30 over Anderson Lake; in slow old steamer which took 3 hours to do some 16 miles; then portage of a mile to Seaton Lake where we had a fast boat which brought us across the lake in 1½ hours. The scenery on this lake is finer than the others, the mountains being higher, steeper & more rugged, decending nearly perpendicularly into the water. The brilliant yellow & red autumn tints contrasting with the dark green & black of the pines, & the bright green of the poplars, together with the varied shades of the rocks were more beautiful than I ever saw before. From Seaton, Milton & Flinn rode in. We loaded a "Lywarle" with our small baggage, & I walked in the 4 miles to Lillooet, a town of one street on one of the terraces of the Fraser. Very fair accommodation at the Stage Hotel

Introduced us to "Judge Elliot", a pleasant little man who had crossed the Atlantic with Milton when he came out to New York before. He invited us to his house & introduced us to Mrs. Elliot, a very ladylike woman, with whom I was rather smitten, having a most remarkable likeness to Mrs. Tylor in both face & manner. In evening met Dr. Walker just arrived from Cariboo.... Very jolly fellow indeed; in Cariboo 5 months; gave us very unpromising news; snow, slush, mire already; not likely to get in with horses if at all. Miners phrases, "You bet," "You bet your gumboots!" "Your bottom dollar," "putting on frills," "piling the agonies," "getting into the mines," & "Caved in," "Played out."

Friday, October 9th— Resolve to go by stage tomorrow. Rather a disturbed night. A half tipsy miner burst into our bedroom & swore it was

The 29 Mile House on the Harrison-Lillooet Road in 1863. There were 13 roadhouses on this route with the 29 Mile the most famous.

Lillooet, from a drawing in the *London Illustrated News*, December 24, 1864. Here Cheadle put his shoes outside his hotel room door, vainly hoping that they would be polished.

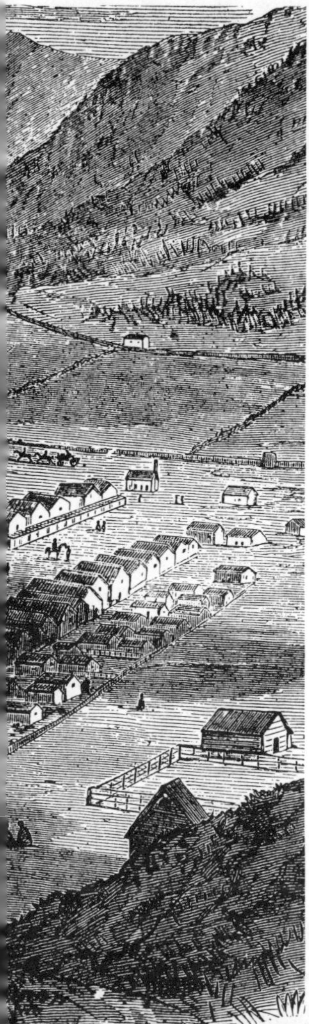

The above sketch from Cheadle's book is of Rattlesnake Grade on 4,000-foot-high Pavilion Mountain where they passed one of the camels used for packing to Cariboo. The photo below shows the last of the animals in the northern Okanagan in 1905.

his, & that it had 3 beds in beforetime. I assured him that it had now only two, & was not his & he made tracks; then at daybreak they rowed us out to ask if we were going on to Seaton by the stage; later on, the bottom of my bed which consisted of nothing but laths nailed on to the frame gave way & I came bump on to the floor, & was compelled to move the mattress on to the floor at the side & try again. Two men passing my door & seeing my boots outside where I had put them in vain hope of their being cleaned a little called out "Who's that d—d d—l, putting on the frills he is?" After breakfast wrote up my notes, & talked with Walker. A poor fellow nearly dying of Cardiac dropsy came in yesterday evening & was very thankful to get me to prescribe for him; better today. Dined with Elliot & met Reverend Brown the parson here, & author of the essay. After leaving there visited Subsheriff Hudson, newly married man; Walker & Flinn there; nice music, "Glorious Apollo" & other glees. "O wert thou in the cauld blast," reminding me of home; not in bed till 12.

Saturday, October 10th—Up at 7, hoping to start at eight & make the 47-mile house (Clinton). But did not leave until 10.30, owing to packing of freight ¾ ton, & only 3 passengers viz. ourselves & Mr. Hall, the Canadian whose horse had foundered over Flinn's ferry and along hilly road mostly cut out of side of mountains & narrow. Our Jehu [driver] a Yankee, drove well & rattled us down the hills; cranky stage, & overweighted, (nearly a ton), & if anything should give way, why, over the precipice. Fraser River scenery. Stayed for night at 15-mile house; wretched place, no fire, no beds. Milton slept under the counter, I alongside it, Hall on the top; 4 or 5 miners along the floor.

Sunday, October 11th—Under way about 7. Passed Judge Begbie on horseback. Everybody praises his just severity as the salvation of Cariboo & terror of rowdies. After about 10 miles come to Captain Marltey's roadside house; has a ranch near & flourishing. Then up the Pavilion mountain with a tremendous ascent, stage road winding along side of hill, but we walked straight up the mountain side, awfully steep & killing; I think 5000 feet above level. Extraordinary appearance of mountain slope on east of creek at bottom, as if waves of land beginning half way down in small waves, & gradually increasing to larger billows towards the bottom. Volcanic eruption or water? 3 miles along level top brought us to 29-mile house where we got fair dinner; passed numerous returning miners & pack trains. Then after ascending still higher, commence descent of Pavilion by "rattlesnake grade", the most dangerus carriage road I ever saw; the road turns 6 times, is very narrow except at the turns, the mountain side terrifically steep. We rattled down at a fearful pace, a wheel coming off, the brake giving way, or a restive horse being almost certain death. At the bottom a lake; at the further end a farm; better land; level road all the way along a valley up to 47-mile house, junction of Lytton & Lillooet roads; several large ranches; only hay, oats, & vegetables grown. Passed a magnificent camel grazing alongside of road; one of the two brought out, first tried in California & then here; failures in both countries. Met Mr. Smith the packer at Clinton; horse given in.

Monday, October 12th—Thro' level country of "cypree" [conifers]

& lakes to 70-mile house for dinner, & forward to 84 to sleep. Miserable teams, horses wretchedly thin & one lame. Passed this morning a curious chasm in the earth 300 or 400 yards wide height 200 or 300 feet perpendicular. Valley sides as if cut with knife, commencing in a gradual depression & ending abruptly in a valley to the south. Passed the stage going down, full; learnt that the horses for next relay at 84 were still lost; therefore no going on beyond there tonight! & the same horses to go on 17 miles tomorrow! Cameron said to be coming down with 540 lbs weight of gold! real weight 630 lbs, 40 or 50 miners on foot; several mule pack trains. Last porter [dark-colored malt beer] at 70-mile house 1¼ dollar per pint bottle!

Tuesday, October 13th—Started late as we had only 16 miles to do. Came on heavy rain, giving us a good soaking before arrival, cleared up after. Afternoon to spend here at 100-mile house for want of horses. Met express waggon here. Express left mouth of Quesnel yesterday morning at 6; since then 60 miles by steamer & 78 by waggon! On the road passed a covered waggon which they told us conveyed a sick miner; found out on our arrival at 100-mile house that it was the man who cut his throat a week ago & had been lying there ever since; now sent down to Lillooet for Doctor. The man is mad. All day thro' high table land thickly wooded with small 'cypree,' sandy, rocky & barren. To 100-mile house descended for nearly 3 miles to low ground; apparently better soil; a little open land & scattered poplars, rather reminding one of the Saskatchewan. Three of the 4 Indians condemned to death for murder of 7 whites (which they confessed) are said to have escaped, their jailor taking them out into the woods with him unfettered, & left them there to wait for his return whilst he went to change his boots. . . .

Wednesday, October 14th—Now out of high land with a series of valleys continued from that of last night, strongly resembling 'park-like' country of Saskatchewan; numerous streams & lakes; hills thickly timbered with pines. Along here many "ranches" where oats, barley & vegetables seem to grow pretty well but very short in the straw. Only these "bottoms" that seem at all likely to repay a farmer. At night passed the spot where Clegg was murdered, not ¼ mile from the next house. Thro' roughish road & down hill to Davidson's (150-mile post), a large square unfinished house; billiard room; lots of geese, ducks & chickens. All kinds of vegetables. Mr. Davidson was exceedingly kind & hospitable, as also Mr. Hudson, brother of the man we met at Lillooet. Gave us some very good Hudson's Bay port to supper. Davidson has an extensive farm here & makes money fast, although he says farming land is not first rate & scarce.

Thursday, October 15th—My Birthday, but I forgot to keep it. A long ride with tired horses; dined at Frank Way's 114-mile, he has farm of valley 4 miles long & ¼ wide; over 200 acres; a considerable part of this growing oats & barley which is cut principally for hay. Then, leaving the valleys, we crossed timbered hills, descending by a sinuous & very steep road into the valley of the Fraser once more at Soda Creek to wait here, where there were a few houses, for the steamer at noon tomorrow. House kept by a Yankee. All 'Docs' & 'Caps'.

Friday, October 16th—Steamer came in about 2'clock bringing a host

At Frank Way's Deep Creek stopping place the two travellers had lunch. At Quesnel, below in the 1860s, they boarded a raft for their memorable journey down the Fraser River to Soda Creek.

Milton and Cheadle discovered that liquor flowed lavishly on the sternwheel steamer *Enterprise*, above at Soda Creek in 1868. Her boilers and other ironware, opposite, are now on display at Quesnel.

of miners 2 of whom were very drunk & continued to imbibe every 5 minutes; during the time we stayed in the house they must have had 20 drinks. The swearing was something fearful. After we had been on board a short time the Captain finding out who we were, gave us the use of his cabin, a comfortable little room, & supplied us with cigars & a decanter of cocktail, also books & papers. We were fetched out every few minutes to have a drink with some one, the Captain taking the lead by standing champagne all round. We had some dozen to do before supper; no one the least affected, Milton & I shirking in quantity. The 'Cap' told us the boat was built on the river, all the timber sawn by hand, the shaft in 5 pieces packed up on mules, cylinders in two, boiler plates brought in same manner. Boat cost $75,000!

Saturday, October 17th—As we did not leave Soda Creek until 4 & the boat makes very slow progress against the powerful current we had to anchor for night after doing only some 10 miles, & then delayed by the dense fogs which prevail on the river in the early morning at this season. Passed Fort Alexander about 10. No great trade there now; depot of furs from the north; 20 miles from Soda Creek. Country more level & under usual Fraser benches, & low wooded hills; river banks sandy; few rocks; River about size of Saskatchewan at Edmonton; Coal found on banks. Continually called out to have a drink.

Sunday, October 18th—Arrived about 9, at Quesnel mouth, a little collection of about 20 houses on the wooded banks of the Fraser. Quesnel at the north side of the Fort. Large new stores & cards all lying about the street. A drizzling rain all day. We made up our pack & set out. Captain Done met us in street half seas over & insisted to treat us to champagne, etc., at every bar in the place. At last escaped & walked to 4-mile house where we found Hall & another man who had started before us waiting for us. We stayed there all night. Packers playing cards. Proprietor one of the Canadians who had come overland & down the Fraser last year. Gave fearful account of hardships especially on the raft.

[The man who rafted down the Fraser River was one of a group of some 150 men, a pregnant woman and her three children who in 1862 trekked from Eastern Canada to the Cariboo. On June 2, 1862, they left Fort Garry (now Winnipeg) in ox-drawn Red River carts. The first 900 miles to Fort Edmonton they covered fairly quickly since they averaged 2½ miles an hour. But for much of the route westward from Fort Edmonton there wasn't even a trail. They abandoned their carts and used horses and oxen as pack animals. At Tete Jaune Cache near Mt. Robson the group split up, some deciding to build huge rafts and challenge the Fraser River, others choosing the Thompson. Several were drowned in the rapid-strewn waterways.

[In all, the overland trek took three months. The venture was summarized by one of them with the words: "Our mining tools were the only articles. . .that we found to be unnecessary." See Heritage House book *The Overlanders of '62*.]

Monday, October 19th—On foot to Smith's, 2 miles beyond the Cottonwood. Awful trail, nothing but stumps, roots & mud up to the ankles.

Saw 6 horses lying dead in the road, hundreds probably a little way off in bush. Thro' nothing but small pines & poplars. Tall 'Maine' man killed 2 martens which crossed the road & we treed, and 2 partridges with his revolver. Very tired and footsore tho' only 20 miles. Milton got thro' famously, walking in moccasins!

Tuesday, October 20th—Sharp frost. Mudholes frozen. Big boots excruciating. Milton & I, each picked up a pair of cast away gumboots on the road & left our own at houses till return; 14 miles to dinner & 6 more after to Beaver Pass where we found the Gold Escort & 40 miners; 12 dead horses & mules on the road. I had an awful cold, sore heels & pack of 30 lbs which I found too heavy before dinner. Awful night last night; wind blowing thro' cracks in walls & floor; only one blanket apiece; 20 men in room; one afflicted with cramp in his leg which brought him on his feet swearing every ½ hour. Milton & another talking in their sleep; rest snoring; my nose running; little sleep.

Wednesday, October 21st—In the morning passed along Lightning Creek to Van Winkle; Milton walked very well; my heels very sore; snow getting deeper up to 3 inches. Called at Irishwoman's named Edwards, 3 miles short of Van Winkle, & had a cup of coffee for which she charged us ½ dollar each. Passed Welsh Company's claim which had stopped working on account of ice having broken wheel. [The "wheel" was a huge waterwheel which ran a pump to keep the mine shaft dry. At Barkerville Historic Park there is a full-size working replica of one.] At Van Winkle about a dozen houses (Lightning Creek). Passed on 2 miles further to a house where we got a capital dinner, beefsteak pie & beefsteak & onions & pancakes! a long weary walk winding along hill sides past the Bald mountain into William's Creek. Milton held out well walking like a man, carrying his hat slung like a pack although there was frost. At dusk we arrived at Richfield, the first part where gold was struck on this creek, & it was quite dark before we reached Cameron Town below, passing thro' Barkerville or Middle town. The whole 3 towns extending almost continuously down the creek for a mile, & containing about 60 or 70 houses apiece. This spring were only 3 or 4 houses at Cameron Town! Our path was a difficult one over endless sluices, flumes & ditches, across icy planks & logs, all getting tumbles, gumboots being very treacherous. Putnam the 'Maine man', took us to his home & treated us, recommending Mr. Cusheon's as a good place to stay at. They gave us a good supper & plenty of blankets.

Thursday, October 22nd—Got up late, being very stiff & sore. In afternoon, Cusheon took us to Cameron Co's hut & introduced us to Steele & the other 3 partners of the Cameron Co. except Cameron & Stevenson who had gone down; they treated us to brandy & water & then took us down to view the operations below. The shaft about 30 feet down thro' gravel & clay to bedrock of slate. Numerous shafts all supported by timber & very closely roofed in with flat crosspieces. Wet, damp, dark & gloomy; the shafts being in many parts very low, the "pay dirt" not being extensive perpendicularly. At the bottom shaft the pay dirt was best high up; at the upper end, down close to the bedrock; they kindly helped us to wash out

Richfield, above, was the first community on Williams Creek, its main street part of the Cariboo Wagon Road.
Barkerville, below, grew around Billy Barker's rich claim which was on a section of Williams Creek the miners originally thought was worthless.

two pans which yielded some beautiful gold to the value of $21, nearly 1⅓ oz; we could see the nuggets lying in the gravel before loosened out by the pick! The claim was bought for a mere nothing, & the thing quite a fluke. Steele showed me about $1000 of gold in a bag, & the Company's books, showing weekly expenses averaging 7000 dollars, the yield being generally from 40 to 112 oz. per shaft (of which there were 3) per day or on to $29,000 per week! over 100 feet of claim yet quite untouched. Steele very kind and intelligent.

Friday, October 23rd—Got up very late, & towards noon walked up the mile to Richfield to see Mr. Cox, a capital fellow. Fat, tall, thick set fellow with very short coat, large features, retiring forehead, no whiskers & large moustache very German; but not in manner. Delicately polite, gentlemanly & jolly. Captain FitzStubbs came in. What a name! had been in army, came out with Barrett Lennard, now speculating in claims. Stayed there until ½ past 4 & on getting back to Cusheon's we found they had eaten our dinner. We had however a very nice one in adjacent house of mother-in-law & daughter who treated us hospitably. Steele invited us to Miner's cabin to have a pipe & we got much information from him.

Saturday, October 24th—FitzStubbs took us to visit the Caledonian claim; did not go down himself for fear of dirtying his coat! Two or three proprietors took us round & helped Milton to wash a pan of dirt which produced nearly an ounce of very coarse gold. The shafts in this mine were very low & wet, the pay dirt being not of great depth. Then had lunch in miners' hut & smoked pipes with them. A large portion of this mine yet unworked. On return were introduced to Mr. Raby, a Cornishman & proprietor of the Raby claim. Also Mr Courtney, a lawyer from Dublin; wonderful number of Irishmen. Raby took us down the "Raby claim" & showed us some rich pockets of gold. The dirt visibly full of it & we could see the 'plums', the bits of gold in the face of the cutting. The place where we found this "pocket" was under a large boulder & this is where they are usually met with. And it is easy to understand how, when the boulder was lying in what was then the bed of the creek, & the water rippling past it, the gold would lodge in the crevices *under* the stone. Mr. Raby picked out a few lumps of the rich dirt, as much as would fill a quart pot perhaps, & Milton washed it. There was about an ounce. The Raby claim is very extensive, 1,000 feet, the pay dirt very extensive, being found high above the bed rock as well as on it, the claim being already worked on drifts 12 feet high in some places; gold has also been found plentifully in the gravel above the drifts & Mr. Raby expects to work this from the surface after the drifts are worked out. Enough to last & pay highly for 3 years. The gold seems evidently to have been washed down the old bed of the stream. The difficulty is to find out where the bed of the creek originally was, & the only way seems to be by following the lead. Claims are sometimes taken up & worked on the present bed, & it is found that the "lead" is not there; it passes right into the hill perhaps on one side or the other of the narrow valley; some slide, or volcanic eruption having changed the course of the stream.

We heard of the Dillon & Currie claim where 102 lbs. of gold were taken out as result of 8 hours work! The Wattie shaft where out of 100 feet of which it consisted $120,000 were taken, leaving over $70,000 clear profit.

Talking to one of the miners, he remarked, "Well, Doctor, I've the greatest respect for both the professions of law & medicine; but its a curious fact that in this creek last year we had neither lawyers nor doctors, & we lived without litigation & free from illness. This year there has been a large influx of both lawyers & doctors, & there has been nothing but lawsuits & deaths in the place!" The appearance of William's Creek (so named from William Dietz, a Prussian, the discoverer) is merely a narrow valley shut in by pine clad hills, the edges & bottom partially cleared & covered with wooden huts, flumes, waterwheels, windlasses, shafts, ditches & tunnels. In the evening went with Stuart, the Cameron Co's. foreman, to see a Scotchwoman who possessed the most beautiful specimen of native gold I have yet seen. Not more than 2 or 3 oz. but like the most perfectly frosted jeweler's gold & of fantastic shape.

Sunday, October 25th—Did but little till afternoon, when Mr. Greer called & took us up to Richfield to call at his cabin to view some 'specimens'. I am already beginning to hate the name. But these were very fine, one nearly 6 oz. the other 7 oz. Both from Loughea; frosted looking bright gold with quartz. He kindly gave us several nice nuggets from the Greer claim on this creek. Introduced to Dr. Black practising here & who promised to go over to Loughea tomorrow with us, 3 miles from this. Dined with "Judge" Cox who was exceedingly pleasant. Present Courtney, a young Canadian,

Janet Morris, who, on October 27, was amongst those who dined with Milton and Cheadle. She spent many hours nursing sick or injured miners, and when she was killed in a horse and buggy accident in 1870, flags in Barkerville were flown at half mast.

& an Englishman whose names I did not catch. A jolly evening, & home by bright moonlight in the snow.

Monday, October 26th—Went over with Black to Loughea. He was very pleasant, having seen a great deal of mining in Australia. Loughea very like William's Creek, only smaller scale; 4 claims working, "Sage Miller", Vaughan, Crane's & another. Pays well, & beautifully fine gold; all done by tunnelling. Milton bought $37 worth of gold from Miller, I contented myself with $10. Miller had been all over the world, California, Australia & up the Amazon which he describes as a magnificent country; found gold (flower) in pan. Had pleasant walk over the hill back to William's Creek 3 miles. The great wants here are capital & steam power. Waterwheels freeze up early. Currie & another are now bringing up engines by the first sleighs. "Mr. Dixie", a nigger barber from Tennessee, was introduced to Milton, & as he said he should die happy if he could only shave a real live lord, he is to operate on Milton tomorrow.

Tuesday, October 27th—Went to Bowling Alley with Cusheon, & he & I licked Milton. Thence to see Mr. Raby of whom Milton bought 2 oz gold & I $10 of specimens. Witnessed washing up of one shaft Raby claim, shift & a half, (15 hours) over $4,000! A preserved meat tin case full.

At 6 went up to the Hospital the other side of the creek on the top of the hill. Found there Courtenay, Mr. Blenkinsopp, an old H.B. Chief Trader now mining, Mr. Cocker, manager of Macdonald's bank here, Dr. Bell, a G.P., Brown, a young Irishman assisting Dr. Black, & Billy Farren, a successful miner in the Caledonia Claim, a rough boisterous Irishman

On the trail Milton and Cheadle met the gold escort, shown at Barkerville in 1863. The escort was formed to ensure safety of gold shipments but wasn't a success because miners preferred Barnard's Express, the firm whose sign is in the background.

who had been a sailor. Also Janet Morris a Scotchwoman, fair, fat & forty, the wife of a man who keeps a store, & who came to make the plum-pudding etc. & of course sat down & dined with us. Champagne ad-lib, & Dr. Bell rapidly became maudlin. He was a little smooth-faced man in dress coat, with large mouth & white teeth always smiling, under some obligation to the FitzWilliam family under whom his father is tenant in Northamptonshire. He rose after the first glass before we had got to pudding & proposed in the most fulsome & absurd manner Milton's health & the Aristocracy of England. "Gentlemen, Dr. Black invited me here to meet a noble scion of the noblest house in England. I don't exaggerate when I say so. I can't exaggerate. I feel grateful to Dr. Black, deeply grateful for asking me here to meet the "noble scion" of one of the noblest houses England ever produced. It is a proud day for all of us & for this creek; it is the commencement of a new era," etc. etc, quite nauseous, & he continued to propose toasts. Interlude, "He's a jolly good fellow" & sentiments, all full of the "Noble Scion". Then Dr. Black overflowing with loyalty, laying his hand upon his heart & willing to die at once for his Queen & country; proposing the health of Her Majesty. Interlude "God save the Queen". My health. Interlude "He's a jolly good fellow" etc. We then adjourned to the kitchen & had more healths; songs. And then Janet presented Milton very prettily with a handsome nugget (25 dollars) for him to give his mother from her. After which in a "gushing" speech Black presented Milton with a large gold ring made on the Creek out of "never sweat" gold worth some $50. Billy Farren then gave me a nice gold & quartz specimen, & Janet another. After all which Dr. Bell essayed several speeches but was sung down by the company in Auld Lang Syne, & after sitting half asleep for some time made a bolt for the door which he thought was next to the chimney, & was led off to bed by Mr. Brown. He rolled off with a crash twice during the evening, cutting his head against the stove. The dinner was held in the Hospital ward, the only patient a poor devil with anascara being covered up with a piece of baize hanging from the wall. We had whist & 7 up pitch, after which supper & hot grog with numerous arguments about the mining laws until two o'clock when I persuaded Milton to come home. Both quite sober.

Wednesday, October 28th—Milton went down another shaft of the Caledonia, & I, sick of going down in buckets, & crouching along drifts, walked on to Richfield & had pipe with the Judge where Milton joined me shortly; we entered into negotiations to borrow $500 from Cox, who was very kind & lent it us gladly; we were already out of cash, having spent $2000 since leaving Victoria, & Cox said that was very moderate indeed! [$200 of this went towards Milton's purchase of land at New Westminster.] To call next day for the money.

Thursday, October 29th—Went with Black to call on 'Janet' & bade her an affectionate goodbye. Introduced to Mr Stenhouse, who had been a man of property in England, ruined by a 'Derby', afterwards made a large fortune as stage coach proprietor in Australia which he again lost, & is now living on speculations & his wits here; a very coarse vulgar but amusing man withal. Volunteers to go down with us tomorrow. Called at the Judge's for cash. Snowstorm; now nearly a foot of snow here, but not cold except

The Barker shaft with Billy Barker at right. The miners went down the shaft in the bucket, with Dr. Cheadle refusing to visit any more mines since he was "Sick of going down in buckets."
From gold yielded by the Neversweat claim, below, Milton had a ring made.

at night when it is down to 5°. In evening Black called & took us into Jem O'B's of the Caledonia to drink whiskey punch.

Friday, October 30th—Bade goodbye to Cusheon & Cameron Town, called & bid adieu to Cox. Our bill for 8 days was 78 dollars each, & very moderate for the place. An Irishman caught us up & walked in company as far as the Edwards 4 miles from Van Winkle. He amused me keeping a constant talk all the way. He was a cattle driver & said he knew the whole country well. Had hunted cattle nearly up to the head of the Fraser & round to Fort George, starting from Antler Creek! a few nights ago in danger from a pack of wolves at Cottonwood. Out on horseback. Climbed into a tree & set fire to the gum etc., & they eventually cleared off. At Edwards we found Stuart (Cameron foreman) & Mathieson (partner in Victoria firm & in claims here); they were on their way to look at two men prospecting the 'Ayrshire Lass' claim on Lightning above on the hill; & we accompanied them down the creek, leaving the trail to the left. Our path lay along the top of the bank above the creek, & in a hollow of what appeared to be the old bed of a stream; at the further end was the 'Ayrshire Lass'; here we found 2 men working at a tunnel into the side of the mountain. Not yet struck the bedrock. They gave up work & led the way down the hill-side into the valley to their cabin. Invited us to stay with them all night as it was already nearly dark, & too late to see the famous Hill diggings that night. We agreed, & they cooked us bacon & beans & with a small bottle of real H.B. Rum given us by John Ducie Cusheon at parting, we spent a very pleasant evening. Adam Ross one of the two, had been a very extensive explorer along Vancouver Island & this coast. Told us 24,000 of one tribe of Indians died last year of small-pox. Turned out into the bush when attacked by the disease, & the men shot themselves & the women hanged themselves; might be seen dead by hundreds; a continual fusillade; awful cold night & only one blanket apiece.

Saturday, October 31st—Bade adieu to our miner friends & went on with Mathieson to view the Butcher & Discovery Claims on the hill; we found men at work on the Butcher, & some sinking a tunnel, others working out from the surface. Could pick out gold from the dirt about a yard below the surface; beautifully fine without quartz & deep yellow. Had all been worked by "hydraulicking", but now too cold, & sluicing used; 200 feet above creek. Old bed of a creek going at right angles into mountain; to be the great excitement next season. Lightning so termed from the Yankee expression, it being very difficult to work, & very uncertain. The lead is lost at every turn of the creek, where it passes round a point. Many claims thus found nothing. It is now supposed that the lead runs thro' the hill at these points, there having been slides which have covered over the original bed. The Hill diggings were discovered by their being at a claim below in the bed of present creek, & finding that the lead evidently did not come down the creek, but from the hill. They tunnelled into the hill to no purpose, but one day one of the boys went on to the top & scratching the earth with his knife saw gold, & on further investigating, it was found in plenty, sometimes 3 or 4 feet only below. Never more than 15 or 16; in Discovery Claim less. Went to Van Winkle for dinner, & then to Welsh Co., 2 miles on. Evans the manager not at home. His son very civil; if there is gold in the creek, they must have it, for they will prospect the whole bottom. Wheel burst with frost, stopping working of shaft; great drawback to Lightning is bed of quicksand; 25 Welshmen employed; backed by Manchester Capitalists.

Sunday, November 1st—Bade goodbye to Mr MacCaffrey & walked on to the Welsh Company's claim. Found Evans Senior at home keeping Sunday. A contrast to William's Creek. He told us that they were now prospecting in the mountains all round & had come upon what he expected would prove a valuable silver lead; no gold; expected to drop upon the "Last Chance" lead with their shaft. Provisions alone had cost $12,000 in 4 months. Had 4 pumps & were completely master of the water in the shaft, which he considered was the main point & which had been the great stumbling block to miners hitherto. Had taken up that claim on Lightning because as the mining laws at present stand the Government cannot grant a lease for a claim over 100 feet unless of ground already worked & abandoned by other miners; therefore he must either take up this large piece of abandoned ground or put himself in the hands of his men by taking up 100 feet in the name of each. But it appears there was enough vacant ground in William's Creek if the law had allowed him to lease it. We passed forward to Beaver Pass for Dinner, 10 miles from Van Winkle & from there 6 miles forward to Edward's. He has been a mate on board a merchant-man for 8 or 9 years, after that mining in Australia, came over here in '58. He is a thorough-going Englishman & gave us several amusing stories of the state

A miner's cabin on Williams Creek in the 1860s. On October 30 Milton and Cheadle spent "a very comfortable evening" in one after a typical supper of bacon and beans.

of things on the first rush to this country. How he was quite alone amongst the Yankees at Boston Bar (or one of the Fraser River Bars); how they bullied him & he gave them tit for tat, they at last rolling him in a ditch & covering him with sand to make an American Citizen of him. We also heard the stories (I forget from whom) of Abbot, the successful Cariboo miner, who shied a handful of 20 dollar pieces at a large pier-glass at Victoria worth some $200, and another who, having treated all the Company in the bar room & finding no more, had all the glasses of the Establishment filled up on the counter, & swept them off with his fist! Another who in the same way being unable to find enough people to treat opened a hamper of champagne & jumped into it, thereby cutting his shins considerably. Major Downie, formerly of Downieville, California, now on William's Creek, at the Christening of Downieville, set up champagne bottles in the ten pin alley & bowled at them! Most of these in fact all are in low water now. Edwards said altho' he hated Yankees, he had the greatest admiration of their energy; they opened out this country in '58 or '59, mostly Southerners; at Boston Bar some of the Yankees got up an excitement, which was agitated by the steamboat proprietor who brought such a report down to Victoria that the Governor sent up Col. Moody & a company of the Engineers in the steamer at once. Steamer stuck on the rapids & was detained a day or two, the owner drawing pay all the time; when they arrived

On October 31 Cheadle visited a claim near Van Winkle on which the "Wheel had burst from frost." The "wheel," shown above on the Davis claim which yielded $350,000, was a water wheel that ran a pump to keep the mine shaft dry.

at the place, there was a great laugh at the expense of the soldiers, the only disturbance which had occurred being between the notorious Ned McGowan & another, in which the former had blackened the eyes of the other. McGowan was fined $25, & the Officers went & had a champagne lunch with him afterwards! 2 Justices of the Peace, one at Yale & and the other at Hope, each decided the cases according as he was paid & constant appeals from one to the other.

Monday, November 2nd—A rough walk from Edward's to Cottonwood, 16 miles. Marten tracks every few yards. Milton & I treed one & fired 6 shots at him with our revolvers without effect. Dined at Smith & Ryder's, & then walked on in heavy snowstorm, to Ramsay's (Cottonwood) for the night. About 20 men there. Got plenty of blankets tho' not very clean. The same amount of snow as at William's Creek.

Tuesday, November 3rd—Very muddy trail to 8-mile house, an Irishman's who gave us a very nice dinner. Chinaman cook. Trapping martens hard; had killed a dozen with a few wretched traps near the house. From there a long 12 miles in to Quesnel mouth; where we arrived after dark; put up at Brown's where they made us very comfortable & gave us whiskey toddy as a nightcap.

Wednesday, November 4th—Steamer [*Enterprise*] stopped & hauled on to the bank — row boat going down tomorrow to Yale which will take us to Soda Creek. Numerous Chinamen keep stores here. Chinese & English signs, Kan See washing, ironing & Bakery, etc. etc. Called on Captain Done on the Steamer. Cocktails every 5 minutes, & champagne lunch afterwards. Happiest man I ever saw. Steward tells me he takes a cocktail every ten minutes when on board. Very jolly fellow. Had to give a keg of brandy to his men before they could haul the steamer on shore. Gave them a champagne dinner on being paid off today, & we heard them singing away below deck. Came in for many champagne drinks during the day. Paid $10 for passage in boat to Soda Creek, & found to our delight & surprise that we had still 3 oz. gold dust to take us forward. Talked with McBride who has been all the season up Peace River thro' the Rocky Mountains a little below Fort St. John. Gold all the way but not in paying quantities on the other side; 7 or 8 men wintering on Peace River. Coarse gold found on Nation River, one of its tributaries. An old Scotchman some 70 years old had found a fine paying claim on that branch. Describes the country as fine farming land. Mixed prairie & timber, lots of game, cariboo tracks like sheep walks, moose, mountain sheep & bears numerous. Immense quantities of fish. Fine salmon trout. Barley & potatoes grow well at Fort George. Also had long conversation with the discoverer of the Bentinck Arm route. He puts the distance from Fort Alexander to Coast at 190 miles, & brought a pack train thro' in 12 days. Lieut. Palmer followed the Indian trail & made it 270, & damned the route. This man however gives a favourable account of the country as being suitable for farming & somewhat resembling the land about Davidson's, etc. Deep Creek; bunch grass & meadow grass in abundance; 30 houses built at Bentinck Arm already. [Today's Bella Coola.] Packers have been running by that route all summer, & one man intends to get grant from Government to make a trail thro' next season.

Here at Quesnel barley & potatoes grow well. The cultivated land has been 'reserved' by Government after being preempted by owners, & no compensation yet given for improvements. Quesnel is on a large flat surrounded by a semicircular range of low hills & on the river bank.

Thursday, November 5th—"Captain" McBride got his boat, a large strongly built 6 oar, ready to start about 11 o'clock & we, together with some 40 other passengers, embarked; very crowded; no room to sit comfortably; like flock of penned sheep. He said he had taken 50 in the same boat last year, & ran thro' to Yale, where he intended to go this time if he could get sufficient passengers. It was a miserably cold, raw, cloudy November day just such as we have in England, & snowing fast, & we were dreadfully starved in spite of several whiskey bottles which came out very soon after we started, & were all emptied before we got very far. The river was unusually low, but we ran all the "riffles" successfully until we came to one below Alexandria, when McBride was induced to take the wrong side by the affirmation of a passenger that the steamer always took that course. Here we stuck fast in a tremendous stream, & could not get her off; there was therefore nothing for it but for some of the men to jump overboard & lighten the boat & help to push her off; several volunteered at once, & carried some of the passengers ashore on their backs, the water being only knee deep. One unfortunate little man got a gigantic miner on his back, & losing his footing, both fell overhead into the water & got thoroughly soused, the small fellow tumbling 3 or 4 times before he could get on his legs against the strong current. Water like ice & day cold enough. Milton & I in the most cowardly manner stuck to the ship & she was quickly lifted over the shallow & taking the drenched men on board again & wrapping them in blankets, we went on until it was almost dark, when the "Cap" suggested camping for the night. Several daredevils urged going forward, but as we were still 10 miles from Soda Creek, & the river so very dangerous, they were overruled by the more sensible, & we put ashore at a large pile of wood belonging to the steamer with which we made free to kindle some enormous fires which were kept going all night. The Captain produced plenty of bread & butter & a flitch of bacon, which with some tea went very well. Milton & I each had a blanket lent us in addition to our own one each, & he constructed a covering of pine boughs, & with my feet to the fire, & a good stock of logs to replenish it, spent a very comfortable night.

Friday, November 6th—Most of the men up before daybreak. Snowing heavily, & I kept my head under the blankets until dawn. We did not start until quite light & made Soda Creek in about an hour. There were several bad places in the river, rock sticking out in the rapids, which made us very thankful we did not try them in the dark. Had breakfast at Soda Creek, left our baggage there for the express to bring forward, & then walked quietly on to Frank Way's (Deep Creek) where we stayed the night. Found the engineer of steamer going down to winter. He told amusing story of the dodges he & Captain Thomas Wright used to work, when in a small underpowered steamer, one of the first on the Fraser running up to Yale. Had a lot of Jew traders on board & heavy freight. Could not get up a riffle. "All passengers overboard to haul at the tow line," shouts Captain

On November 8 Cheadle walked through the snow to the south end of Williams Lake to visit a farm. At the north end was the Pinchbeck farm, today the site of the community of Williams Lake.

Teamsters, their covered wagons and two Express stagecoaches at Bonaparte House, today's Cache Creek. The scene was a familiar one to Milton and Cheadle on their journey down the just completed Cariboo Wagon Road.

Wright. Not a man would stir. "How much steam on, engineer?" shouts the Captain. "175 lbs., sir, already," replies he with great seriousness. "Then put on 25 lbs., more & blow her to h—ll," cries the Captain. "Aye, aye, Sir," responds engineer; this used to be quite enough for the Jew passengers; & overboard went every man like a shot & hauled up the steamer. Thus they made up for want of power.

Saturday, November 7th—Walked forward to Davidson's (Lake Valley Farm) 14 miles. Met Todd the Canadian Horse keeper at [Fort] Kamloops with a Company's pack train for [Fort] Alexandria. Told us that . . . Martin was all right but Burgess had been blown up in the boat, only small pieces of either man or boat found; no one knew how it happened. Matches packed next to powder kegs & perhaps thus. Poor Burgess! quiet hardworking fellow.

Davidson down in Victoria but Hudson in charge, very kind; resolve to wait here a day or two for Express.

Sunday, November 8th—Walk 3 miles down to head of William's Lake to see the farm. Only good land at bottom of perhaps a thousand acres. Some of barley sown late & small on account of drought. Earlier sown very fine. Farm only commenced in spring. Cabbages very fine; potatoes good. Wheat sown for experiment, but looked very small, weak, & yellow. These bottoms are the only land worth cultivation in British Columbia; all the rest rocky & dry, only producing bunch grass. And the alluvial valleys are not very numerous or of large extent. Pumpkins & squashes of large size. Cattle look very fat & well. Calves bred on the place particularly good.

Monday, November 9th—Tried shooting but found no grouse; ducks too wild. Read newspapers by last Express.

Tuesday, November 10th—Took walks & talked of music with Hudson. . . .

Wednesday, November 11th—Hear from men coming down that Express will be several days yet. Heigh ho; rather wearisome altho' first rate feed & cookery; nigger cook up to anything.

Thursday, November 12th—Mulatto came in with nice specimen of gold from Horse Fly Creek about 35 miles from here; one of the tributaries into lower head of Quesnel lake. Coarse scaly gold of beautiful quality. Paid tolerably well, \$2 to \$10 to the pan. Not many men working there.

[On Horse Fly Creek, today the Horsefly River, the first gold in the Cariboo was mined in June 1859 by Peter Dunlevey, Tom Manifee, Jim Sellers and Tom Moffit. While the men were prospecting at the junction of the Chilcotin and Fraser Rivers they were told by a friendly Indian named Tomaah that for generations his people had picked up on the creek nuggets the size of beans. Tomaah then led the whites some fifty miles eastward to the area.]

Friday, November 13th—On Wednesday Frank Way came in for surgical assistance, having in a drunken row with an Irishman had his lower lip almost bitten off, & a finger to the bone. I stitched it up for him, making a very neat job. Foolishly refused any fee. . . .

Set to work & dried the barley still out, the weather being very fine & windy, the snow almost gone, quite hot in the sun, & slight frost at night. September or October weather of England.

Saturday, November 14th—A number of men arrived on way down from William's Creek. Came down in canoes. One laden to water's edge with 14 men swamped in rough water of first riffle 2 miles below Quesnel; 7 men lost; of the others, 5 clung to canoe & got ashore, one was thrown on beach by an eddy, with money & blankets all safe. Another swam ashore, but obliged to drop his blankets containing the dust when within a few yards; 3 or 4,000 dollars lost; 5 belonging to Prince of Wales claim. Adam Ross (in whose cabin we stopped on Lightning Creek) told us that his partner (who we also met there) was one of those lost altho' a good swimmer. He delayed a day at the mouth in order to try & get a companion to go by Bentinck Arm & thus escaped. I remember the riffle well, a tremendous rush of water & very rough so that even our large boat shipped water. Frank Way came back to have his lip redressed. Went off into a fit of laughter the other night & sutures gave way. Milk punch instituted with great success.

Sunday, November 15th—Milton & Hudson rode over to Briggs 6 miles towards Deep Creek where the latter had business. Came back seedy from bad claret. I mooned about the farm. Barley drying well.

Monday, November 16th—Frank Way came over with horses for thrashing machine. Barley thrashed out altho' very wet. Express waggon came in to our great delight. Poole very sorry he had not met us, (being at Alexander when we passed in the boat) for he would have given us a waggon & pair to drive ourselves down to Yale, & we should have been in Victoria by this time. Bad luck; 18 inches snow on William's Creek; none at Quesnel Mouth.

Tuesday, November 17th—Poole the Express man had to go down to William's Lake (Mimion Ranch) 11 miles, & came back this morning. Found Gompertz (who had charge of Post Office, & constable over 7 Indians, 3 of whom are under sentence of death, & the other 4 suspected of the crime) too drunk to read the letter. A Klootcheman with him as drunk as himself. Under constable equally drunk with Sywash & Klootcheman in company. Nice state of things, eh! Bid adieu to Hudson after dinner. One fellow passenger a Captain Harrison who told us he left England 20 years ago intending to return every year since & never been able. Been all over Coast of South America, Honolulu, Australia, New Zealand. Now interested in Cariboo, & partner in proposed bed rock flume.

Arrived at dark Blue Tent, 23 miles, after very cold drive. Hail storm & tremendous wind; heard trees falling all round like cannonade.

Wednesday, November 18th—Off before day light; breakfast at Anderson's 10 miles on Lake La Hache. At Bridge Creek (27 miles) by dinner; from there, leaving the mixed & open country like Davidson's which extends from Bridge Creek to Frank Way's (Deep Creek), we pass up right on to the mountain of green timber at considerable elevation which lasts for 53 miles, nearly to Junction. The road here was covered with ice, & we had to walk up the hill. One horse came down, & we had to unlimber

Ashcroft Manor, built in 1863, still stands, an excellent example of a pioneer roadhouse. It is now a museum.

C.F. Cornwall, one of the two brothers who founded Cornwall Ranch.

Below: The Clinton Hotel in 1863. It became a familiar landmark, serving the public for almost a century until it burned in 1958.

& help up the hill by pushing behind; took us till 8 to get to 84-mile house; we had hoped to reach 74 (Loch Lomond, the old Sergeant's); very severe for horses.

Thursday, November 19th—Overslept & had breakfast before starting. Road a sheet of ice covered with a few inches of snow. Horses frequently down; had to help the waggon up the steep hills. Met Express coming up at 79-mile post & changed drivers, going forward to Loch Lomond, Sergeant McMurphy's, dined there, & afterwards only got to 59-mile house. Began to snow heavily before we got in. Man went out & shot wolf prowling round.

Friday, November 20th—Up at 5.30, starting at daybreak to 47-mile House (Clinton Cut-Off Valley) for breakfast. Fearfully cold; 6 inches of snow during night. Arrived about 10. Horses done, & our feet almost frozen. A lot of teamsters & packers at the "Hotel", drinking & one proposed as a toast "The American Eagle which whipped Great Britain, spat on France, p....d on Spain & Portugal...." with a brick bat afterwards. We were glad to get away from the noise. We did not get off until 3 o'clock, then had 30 miles to do. We had fine moonlight & got to Cornwall's Ranch about 9 o'clock. They have 2 houses, one wayside kept by an employee & their own farm house some ½ mile distant.

The Chinaman cook had got to bed & turned out very sulky to provide us with beefsteaks — our fellow passenger Captain Harrison would have toast which added to his ill-temper. The younger Cornwall (the elder being down at Victoria for supplies) sent word down that he would be glad to see us at the other house & Milton & I walked up there after supper. Found a tall regular First-Trinity man who received us very hospitably. Had evidently been much disappointed with the country & agriculture. He said some barley had turned out very well; the rest badly; irrigation required. Has got post holes dug for some 3 miles; land open, bunch grass country, either sand or gravel, & I feel certain will never pay for cultivation. They are now going in for Stock farming which will do well if bunch grass lasts. He took his degree in 1859; came out here April 1862.

[In 1862 C.F. and H.P. Cornwall started Cornwall Ranch which became one of the best known in the Interior, with Clement Cornwall becoming Lieutenant-Governor of B.C. in 1881.

[The first 150 cattle they purchased for $10 each at Coeur D'Alene, Idaho. Bringing them home "only" entailed a drive across the State of Washington, then some 200 miles up the Okanagan Valley, over the hills to swim across the Thompson River and, finally, into home pasture. The gold rush stimulated sales and the cattle were sold at a good profit.

[Two English traditions that the brothers maintained were horse racing and fox hunting. The horse races on Cornwall Flats attracted upwards of 1,000 spectators from all over B.C., most arriving on horseback or by stagecoach. When English thoroughbreds failed to satisfy the sporting brothers' demands, they imported an Arabian stud.

[The fox hunts — actually coyotes — were conducted with the same pomp and ceremony as in England. The illusion was heightened by having Indians dressed in red coats. Their main duty was opening and closing gates as the boisterous hunters charged across farm and field. Every effort was

At Yale, above in the 1860s, the travellers caught a sternwheel steamer for Victoria. Yale remained the portal to Cariboo until construction of the CPR in the early 1880s destroyed the Cariboo Wagon Road.
St. John's Church, near left center in the photo, was built in 1860 and is still in use.

made to procure the best hounds, even to having special dogs shipped around Cape Horn in sailing ships.

[In 1862 the brothers built a flour mill and a stopping place they called Ashcroft Manor. In the days when roadside hostels were so rough and dirty that some discerning travellers preferred to sleep in the fields, Cornwall's was described as "the quietest, most comfortable hotel on the road with lots of English papers lying around the rooms." The original building also served as the first courthouse in the area, as well as a store and post office.

[The Manor still serves the public, although not as a hostel. It is now a museum where visitors can turn back the clock well over a century and see how travellers were accommodated in the early 1860s. The two large elms in front of the building were brought as seedlings from England and are now over 100 years old.]

Saturday, November 21st—Went off without disturbing our host & drove over to Cook's Ferry [today's Spences Bridge] for dinner. The road for 3 or 4 miles some few miles before the ferry passes round some high rocky bluffs. The dangerous trail we rode over when coming down before, the road being then not finished. It is now only 12 feet wide professedly; in many parts really much less from sliding down of the steep sides above the road partially blocking it; the pole was loose, spring broken, waggon generally very loose, traces continually coming off, no brake, heavy load (170 lbs. gold, 4 passengers & luggage) 2 small horses very tired; road very steep up to point of bluff, & then ditto down, about width of waggon, sheer descent of 600 or 700 feet into rocky bed of Thompson, perpendicular side of mountain above; a restive horse or any breakage certain destruction. Part of the road last made by the Engineers (when L. Palmer was anxious to get away to be married) was a narrow strip of loose sand, built up at the edge by loose stones which had partly given way; an awful place. We crossed carefully & safely. Arrived at Cook's Ferry for dinner, after which drove within 10 miles of Lytton; similar road but wider; same precipices & steeps; waggon pole dropped lose, fortunately when we were on the level; tied him up again.

Sunday, November 22nd—Arrived in Lytton to breakfast. Met Captain Ball again. Parson came up from Yale to hold service in the Court house, but no notice had been given, & no congregation could be got altho' vigorous efforts were made by sending a Sywash round as bellman. Nearly all French & French Canadians in Lytton. . . .

Went forward 15 miles for night horses being too tired to do more; leaving 47 miles to do tomorrow.

Monday, November 23rd—Boston Bar to breakfast; 17 miles; quite a little town; same style of road. Had been well-to-do in river digging ore; now a miserable hole. Delayed a long time there feeding horses; reached bridge 14 miles above Yale a little after dark. On leaving here a few hundred yards the waggon completely broke down, the iron stanchions giving way and pole & cross bars tumbling to ground; on level road; wonderful luck; if this had happened on a precipice we should probably have been lost. Fortunately the other waggon belonging to Express was at the bridge with a splendid pair of horses, Smith's of Cottonwood who was taking some goods up in it. Humphreys, therefore went back for them, whilst we stayed to guard the treasure. We lighted a good fire in the road which served to amuse us until Humphreys returned with other waggon & extra horses which we hitched on in front. Humphreys had brought a bottle of brandy & was greatly exhilarated, had never driven 4 in hand before. Off we went, however we went rattling down hill along the edge of precipices at an awful pace. Humphreys holding reins, Smith sitting beside, whipping up & passing the brandy. Milton & I were in a funk at first, but seeing that the leaders took all the turns to perfection without guiding, felt relieved & half dozed into Yale where we arrived at ½ past 10, having come the 14 miles in about 2 hours. Had supper of tough old fowls, & then turned in about 1. Canyons above Yale very fine. Large rocks stand out in the middle of river.

Tuesday, November 24th—On board 'Reliance', having borrowed $30 from Alard, H.B. Co.'s officer in charge there. Arrived at New Westminster about 6. Called on Captain Spalding, very demonstrative. Abused Colonel Moody & told very long wearisome yarns about tigers & serpents in India. Mrs. S. vainly endeavouring to break the spell. Went on board 'Enterprise' for night in a pouring rain.

Wednesday, November 25th—Not off till 12, full of passengers. Very rough thro' Gulf of Georgia; several sick; I had to retire & assume recumbent posture to quieten sundry qualms. After became still & dined in peace. No cash left. Purser refused to take our fare, the H.B. Co. magnificently

Victoria in the 1860s and the city's 300-pound mayor, Thomas Harris.

granting free passage again. Captain Mowatt came to warn me against our travelling friend Captain Harrison whom he stated was rather disreputable; a kind of male pimp from what I could make out. We reached Victoria at 6.30 & went to St. George's where we were rapturously welcomed by Mrs. Bendixen. Had bath & went to Theatre where we saw tragedy of Camille, a version of Lady of Camellias, much overdone by Mrs. Dean Hayne. Milton then adjourned to the 'Fashion' and I to bed.

Thursday, November 26th—Not up till noon! Spent day in reading papers & shopping as required much refitting. Milton went to Lyceum, I remained to Journalise & read.

Friday, November 27th—Called on Governor [Douglas] who kept us to dine. Begbie & Captain Martley also there. Begbie very fine, a fine tall fellow of 6 feet, well made & powerful, magnificent head, hair scanty & nearly white, with nearly black moustache & beard, full of wit. I was much taken with him. 'Sir James' was very kind, & Lady Douglas homely & good natured.

Saturday, November 28th—Invited to St. Andrews Society's dinner on Monday. Dined with Good (Governor's son-in-law, & an Official of B.C.). Played Vingt-et-un till midnight.

Sunday, November 29th—Called on the Mayor concerning steamer 'Emily Harris' for Nanaimo; to sail on Tuesday. Lascelles sent word we had better delay until the 'Forward' which he would take there when the next mail came in, & we decided to do so as being much pleasanter.

Monday, November 30th—Business all day with H.B. Company & our

Victoria's California Saloon in the 1860s. Milton's favorite was the Fashion, but no photos of it seem to have survived

debts, etc., dining with St. Andrews Society in evening; hiring full dress from tailor. Very mild affair. Retired after set toasts & played whist soberly in Begbie's rooms till 4 a.m. Milton going round of town with Lascelles.

Thursday, December 3rd—Idled about, Milton being seedy & I looking after him. . . .

Friday, December 4th—Dined with the Mayor [Thomas Harris, a huge man who weighed 300 pounds]. ("Madame Bendixen" inveighed against the degradation of dining with 'le gros boucher'); Harris is a butcher & commenced life here by borrowing 2 sheep from the H.B. Company & selling mutton retail in a tent. The Attorney General Cary was there & ended very drunk. We sat 5 hours & never joined the ladies.

PUBLISHER'S NOTE: Milton and Cheadle left Victoria on December 20 by boat for Panama. Here they crossed the Isthmus by land — the Panama Canal was still some 50 years in the future — then continued by water to England via New York.

Dr. Cheadle completed his very successful book then returned to medicine. His career was a long and distinguished one. He was Dean of St. Mary's Medical School from 1869 to 1873, and among the early supporters of allowing women to study medicine. In fact, Cheadle was one of the first professors to lecture at the London School of Medicine for Women. In 1866 he married Anne Murgatroyd and they had four sons.

Unfortunately, Anne died at an early age and in 1884 he married again but his second wife also predeceased him. Dr. Cheadle died in 1910 at 75. In addition to his books, he was the author of many papers on children's health, a field in which he had specialized.

Lord Milton, by contrast, was fated for a short life. He lived only 13 years after their return to England, dying in 1877 at 38.

The "mere party of pleasure" as Dr. Cheadle described themselves are commemorated by Mount Milton and Mount Cheadle between Blue River and Valemount in the North Thompson Valley. This is the region where in 1863 they were 6 weeks fighting through 180 miles of wilderness between Mt. Robson and Fort Kamloops and almost died of starvation. Over Highway 5 the same journey is now an easy 4-hour drive.

Highway 5 north of Blue River near Mt. Cheadle.

A selection of other HERITAGE HOUSE titles:

The PIONEER DAYS IN BRITISH COLUMBIA Series
Every article is true, many written or narrated by those who, 100 or more years ago, lived the experiences they relate. Each volume contains 160 pages in large format magazine size (8½ x 11), four-color covers, some 60,000 words of text and over 200 historical photos, many published for the first time.

A continuing Canadian best seller in three volumes which have sold over 75,000 copies. Each volume, $12.95

WHITE SLAVES OF THE NOOTKA
On March 22, 1803, while anchored in Nootka Sound on the West Coast of Vancouver Island, the *Boston* was attacked by "friendly" Nootka Indians. Twenty-five of her 27 crew were massacred, their heads "arranged in a line" for survivor John Jewitt to identify. Jewitt and another survivor became 2 of 50 slaves owned by Chief Maquina, never knowing what would come first ---- rescue or death.

The account of their ordeal, published in 1815, remains remarkably popular. New Western Canadian edition, well illustrated. 128 pages. $9.95

THE DEATH OF ALBERT JOHNSON: Mad Trapper of Rat River
Albert Johnson in 1932 triggered the greatest manhunt in Canada's Arctic history. In blizzards and numbing cold he was involved in four shoot-outs, killing one policeman and gravely wounding two other men before being shot to death.

This revised, enlarged edition includes photos taken by "Wop" May, the legendary bush pilot whose flying skill saved two lives during the manhunt. Another Canadian best seller. $7.95

OUTLAWS AND LAWMEN OF WESTERN CANADA
These true police cases prove that our history was anything but dull. Chapters in 160-page Volume Three, for instance, include Saskatchewan's Midnight Massacre, The Yukon's Christmas Day Assassins, When Guns Blazed at Banff, and Boone Helm — The Murdering Cannibal.

Each of the three volumes in this Canadian best seller series is well illustrated with maps and photos, with four-color photos on the covers. Volume One, $9.95; Volume Two, $8.95; Volume Three, $10.95

B.C. PROVINCIAL POLICE STORIES: Mystery and Murder from the Files of Western Canada's First Lawmen
The B.C. Police, born in 1858, were the first lawmen in Western Canada. During their 90 years of service they established a reputation as one of the most progressive police forces in North America. All cases in these best selling titles are reconstructed from archives and police files.
Volume One: 16 chapters, many photos, 128 pages. $9.95
Volume Two: 22 chapters, many photos, 144 pages. $9.95
Volume Three: 23 chapters, many photos, 160 pages. $12.95

B.C. BACKROADS
This best selling series contains complete information from Vancouver through the Fraser Canyon to Cache Creek, east to Kamloops country and north to the Cariboo. Also from Vancouver to Bridge River-Lillooet via Whistler. Each book contains mile-by-mile route mileage, history, fishing holes, wildlife, maps and photos.

Volume One — Garibaldi to Bridge River Country-Lillooet. $9.95
Volume Three — Junction Country: Boston Bar to Clinton. $9.95
Thompson-Cariboo: Highways, byways, backroads. $4.95

An Explorer's Guide: MARINE PARKS OF B.C.
To tens of thousands of boaters, B.C.'s Marine Parks are as welcome and convenient as their popular highway equivalents. This guide includes anchorages and onshore facilities, trails, picnic areas, campsites, history and other information. In addition, it is profusely illustrated with color and black and white photos, maps and charts.

Informative reading for boat owners from runabouts to cabin cruisers. 200 pages $12.95.

GO FISHING WITH THESE BEST SELLING TITLES

HOW TO CATCH SALMON — BASIC FUNDAMENTALS
The most popular salmon book ever written. Information on trolling, rigging tackle, most productive lures, proper depths, salmon habits, downriggers, where to find fish, and much more.

Sales over 130,000. 176 pages. $5.95

HOW TO CATCH SALMON — ADVANCED TECHNIQUES
The most comprehensive advanced salmon fishing book available. Over 200 pages crammed full of how-to-tips and easy-to-follow diagrams. Covers all popular salmon fishing methods: mooching, trolling with bait, spoons and plugs, catching giant chinook, and a creel full of other information.

A continuing best seller. 192 pages. $11.95

HOW TO CATCH CRABS: How popular is this book? This is the 11th printing, with sales over 90,000. $4.95

HOW TO CATCH BOTTOMFISH: Revised and expanded. $5.95

HOW TO CATCH SHELLFISH: Updated 4th printing.
144 pages. $3.95

HOW TO CATCH TROUT by Lee Straight, one of Canada's top outdoorsmen. 144 pages. $5.95

HOW TO COOK YOUR CATCH: Cooking seafood on the boat, in a camper or at the cabin. 8th printing. 192 pages. $4.95

FLY FISH THE TROUT LAKES
with Jack Shaw
Professional outdoor writers describe the author as a man "who can come away regularly with a string when everyone else has been skunked." In this book, he shares over 40 years of studying, raising and photographing all forms of lake insects and the behaviour of fish to them.

Written in an easy-to-follow style. 96 pages. $8.95

SALMON FISHING BRITISH COLUMBIA: Volumes One and Two
Since B.C. has some 7,000 miles of coastline, a problem to its 400,000 salmon anglers is where to fish. These books offer a solution. Volume One includes over 100 popular fishing holes around Vancouver Island. Volume Two covers the Mainland Coast from Vancouver to Jervis Inlet. Both include maps, gear to use, best times, lures and a tackle box full of other information.

Volume One — Vancouver Island. $9.95
Volume Two — Mainland Coast: Vancouver to Jervis Inlet. $11.95

Heritage House books are sold throughout Western Canada. If not available at your bookstore you may order direct from Heritage House, Unit 8, 17921 55 Ave., Surrey, B.C. V3S 6C4. Payment can be by cheque or money order but please add $1.00 a book to help pay postage and handling.
